Interview Answers

Detailed Guide on How to Get Any Job You Want. The Perfect Answers to Every Interview Question & Success Tips to Master the Job Interview Process and Be Hired

Table of Contents

Introduction

Chapter 1: Getting Ready for the Big Interview

Chapter 2: Facing the Popular Questions

Chapter 3: Tackling Queries on Education

Chapter 4: Keep It Professional

Chapter 5: The 'Why' Question

Chapter 6: The Unusual Questions!

Chapter 7: A Whole Bunch of Answers!

Chapter 8: The Illegal Questions!

Conclusion

© Copyright 2019 - All rights reserved.

The follow eBook is reproduced below with the goal of providing information that is as accurate and reliable as possible. Regardless, purchasing this eBook can be seen as consent to the fact that both the publisher and the author of this book are in no way experts on the topics discussed within and that any recommendations or suggestions that are made herein are for entertainment purposes only. Professionals should be consulted as needed prior to undertaking any of the action endorsed herein.

This declaration is deemed fair and valid by both the American Bar Association and the Committee of Publishers Association and is legally binding throughout the United States.

Furthermore, the transmission, duplication or reproduction of any of the following work including specific information will be considered an illegal act irrespective of if it is done electronically or in print. This extends to creating a secondary or tertiary copy of the work or a recorded copy and is only allowed with an expressed written consent from the Publisher. All additional rights reserved.

The information in the following pages is broadly considered to be a truthful and accurate account of facts, and as such any inattention, use or misuse of the information in question by the reader will render any resulting actions solely under their purview. There are no scenarios in which the publisher or the original author of this work can be in any fashion deemed liable for any hardship or damages that may befall them after undertaking information described herein.

Additionally, the information in the following pages is intended only for informational purposes and should thus be thought of as universal. As befitting its nature, it is presented without assurance regarding its prolonged validity or interim quality. Trademarks that are mentioned are done without written consent and can in no way be considered an endorsement from the trademark holder.

Introduction

If people were to honestly jot down a list of moments or events that make them feel slightly unhinged and uncomfortable, it would be no surprise that facing an interview would be somewhere at the top. There is no second opinion about it because going through the process of interviews is quite tricky and tends to unnerve even the calmest of profiles and candidates. All it takes is one question that they "did not see coming," and immediately, all that effort and hard work just go to waste.

Facing interviews is one thing; the real difficulty lies in answering the questions raised by the interviewer. Questions as simple as "Tell me a bit about yourself" are mismanaged, wrongly answered, and sometimes, not even answered at all. These questions are designed to test the true potential of the candidate, and unfortunately, quite a lot of us fail to capitalize on the opportunity.

"Interview Answers" is your doorway to success. If you are expecting an interview a few days from now, rest assured that after a little practice and a good read through this book, you will walk through those doors brimming with confidence and equipped with every possible trait in the book. At no point during this book should you consider yourself as weak or ineligible or underestimate your potential in any way. Surely, you have something that the employer has identified, and based upon that element, a decision was made to call you in for an interview. Well done there!

Now that you have that out of the way, let this book take you through real-life examples to learn just how people can ensure they get the job they truly want. We will look through various questions and their possible answers.

We won't just claim that this book is different; we will prove it by presenting various answers to cover different situations. Normally, you'd find one answer, and that would be that. Let's be honest, not everyone has previous job experience nor the confidence to speak or even elaborate on their skills in the right manner. Every candidate holds something unique. We will try and take some common situations and ensure that appropriate answers from each of these situations are provided so that the readers have something to relate to and can prepare for the upcoming interview accordingly.

A fresh graduate, who may be full of hopes and dreams, may have never faced a job interview before. His approach to the subject and the questions would ideally be different from the people who have some job experience and have faced a number of interviews before. While writing this book, such aspects were taken into consideration, and appropriate answers were provided. It is encouraged that you read all the answers as they might provide you with some inspiration to further enhance your delivery of words and cement yourself as the ideal candidate for the job.

Before We Begin

There are a few things that are both recommended and essential that you need to keep in mind before we move on to the actual book itself.

To make the most out of this book, it is recommended that you practice your communication skills frequently. You may complete the book and have all the possible variations of the answers you need to deliver, but if you cannot effectively convey them, they will serve you no purpose at all.

To practice your communication skills, stand before a mirror and say the answers out loud like you would during the interview. It greatly helps to have confidence and positive body language as that adds character and charisma. Maintain eye contact with yourself and try not to break the eye contact.

This may seem odd and rather strange at first, but soon you will realize just how helpful this exercise will be once you have your interview.

There are quite a lot of tips to remember, but those are either based on certain situations or during delivery of answers only. The above, however, will help you out throughout your interview, public speaking sessions, or meetings where all eyes will be on you.

The essence of this exercise is:

- To build up confidence
- To learn where you may lose momentum and how to correct that
- To analyze the answers
- To learn how to be comfortable when maintaining eye contact
- To enhance body language and gestures
- To identify other areas of improvement like facial expressions, posture, and more

Our goal, by the end of this book, is to prepare you for almost all interviews in the future. Most of these will contain generic questions; however, if you belong to a technical field, expect some technical questions to arise. We will try and look into some examples for such fields as well so that you will have an idea of what it would be like to face such questions and then come up with answers in the shortest margin of time.

While the interview style might vary from position to position, generally, you will encounter a single individual conducting your interview in most cases. If you are applying for higher positions, such as senior manager, regional manager, or a director position, expect a full panel to be seated before you. As nerve-wracking as this may sound, there is nothing for you to worry about. As long as you come prepared for the interview, there is nothing to fear, nothing that will be asked of you that may seem out of the ordinary.

For our technical friends specializing in fields like computer science, medicine, engineering, and so on, you may be facing roughly the same question. This book is written to accommodate all such aspects that apply universally. For questions like "Can you tell the difference between a 'function' and a 'method'?" you will need to rely on specialized experience or education to get yourself through. This falls outside the scope of this book and, hence, will not be covered.

It takes practice to master these answers. You should not expect to remember each one of these word for word. Doing so is both counter-productive and goes completely against the idea of 'teaching' yourself how to master interview questions and answers. Keep an open mind and try to analyze the central idea of the answers. You may wish to modify these according to your situation to make them more relevant.

There is no such thing as a 'shortcut' for success, but this book does take the element of surprise away to ensure you are well prepared and comfortable whenever you are presented with a question. If you follow the tips accordingly, you are very likely to walk out as a candidate who truly made an impression.

The Answers Alone Do Not Guarantee You a Job

An interview is all about getting to know you better. As we learned earlier, acquiring all the knowledge from this book will serve you no purpose if you have not understood how to apply the said knowledge correctly.

If, during the interview, you fail to answer questions on time or you end up freezing, which is a lot more common than people will admit, you will only put yourself in a spot of trouble, and the prospect of acquiring said job will immediately become a far-fetched dream.

Ensure that you continue practicing these skills and learn exactly how you can apply the knowledge for each given situation. The book does not guarantee you a job just based on an interview. There are quite a lot of other elements that lie outside the scope of this book, such as your credentials, previous experiences, your references, and any previous charges or records against your name. The book is designed to walk you through the phase of the interview with promising results. All the situations described or discussed within the book are based on assumptions that every candidate has all the prerequisites fulfilled such as a relevant degree and has no prior criminal record. Where necessary, we will differentiate between the answers given by someone who is experienced and someone who has never worked before, which makes the prior experience an advantage, not compulsory in nature.

With that said, take the time now to sit back and begin your journey to master the art of interviews by gaining insights, tips, tricks, and recommendations about what you should say when posed with a mountain of questions.

Chapter 1: Getting Ready for the Big Interview

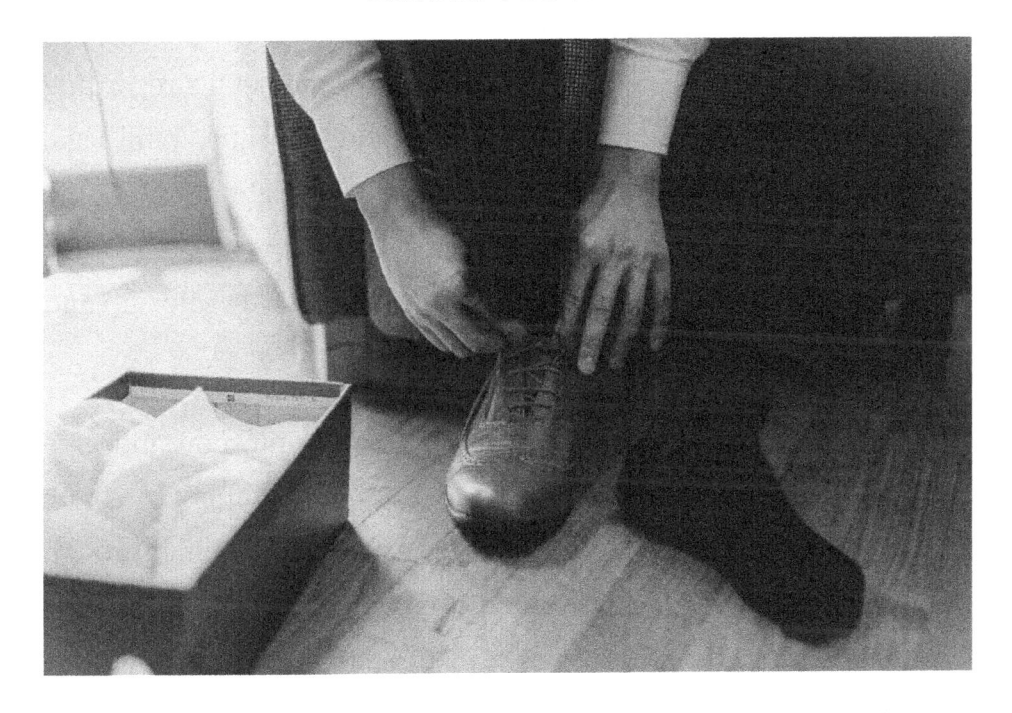

One fine day, you are doing your regular activities at home when you decide to look at jobs. You go online and start browsing the various job openings. You have done this a number of times already, and pretty much every post that comes through you have applied to already.

Feeling a bit under the weather, you are about to call it a day. Just as you get up, your phone rings. The number isn't familiar, perhaps another one of those sales calls; you decide to answer it anyway.

The friendly, courteous voice of a female from the other end asks to confirm if she is speaking to you. Upon confirmation, she informs you that you are scheduled for an interview and that you should soon be receiving an email with all the details regarding the venue, the date of the interview, and the time. While she continues to talk a little more about what you might need to bring with you, you are taken completely over by joy. You finally broke the ice and got yourself a job interview. You quickly catch up and end the call.

A joyous shout or two later, you turn your laptop on and glue yourself to the screen and wait for that magical email to come. Sure enough, it arrives! Your eyes eagerly start scrolling through the email, and you ensure you note everything down accordingly. You set in the coordinates on your phone's GPS, you memorize the time, set the alarms, and make a quick checklist for all the documents you need to bring with you to the interview.

So far, so good. The rest of the day goes by rather quickly, and before you know it, your interview draws closer by 24 hours. Now, the slight uneasiness starts to creep in.

"You are scheduled for an *interview.*"

The feeling only grows stronger as time goes by. Before you realize it, it will be D-day, and you will have done absolutely nothing to prepare for the interview. It will not matter if you have done a few interviews before or not; there are far too many things that can and will go wrong.

By the time you approach the front desk, your heart is beating a little too fast. You can feel it pounding hard within your chest. You confirm your attendance and sign the guest register to obtain your visitor's card. As you wait, you look around the hall and see other candidates. Some are more appropriately dressed while others seem to brim with confidence. Some are engaged in a healthy conversation with each other, and that person in the corner is perfectly well-poised and relaxed. You, on the other hand, are none of that!

Eventually, they leave one by one. The guy who seemed confident came back with a puzzled look. The two candidates who were speaking to each other returned bewildered. The guy who was well-dressed came out with the same blank face he had before. Now, it's down to you and the other guy.

Stop right here!

We don't want to proceed ahead at all. It is obvious that we will not end up with the job. However, the reason we are stopping here is to analyze what went wrong leading up to now. We haven't even gotten to the part where we greet the interviewer, let alone the actual interview itself. Already, we are clearly suffering.

What we have above is a recipe for a disastrous first impression. We are clearly not ready, not well-dressed; we have no idea what the company does or what they will be expecting in the interview. We were so busy with our daily routines and enjoying the fact that we received an interview call that we overlooked the most elementary step of them all: preparation.

Preparing for the Interview

Every now and then, you may come across a little humor. It is done deliberately to liven up the mood a little. With that said, we are preparing for an interview, not a battle of the goliaths.

Interview preparations go far beyond just "dressing to impress" and arriving on time. Those are, indeed, vital elements, but the real struggle comes before that. Let's go back to the email situation we read about just a minute or so ago and restart the story, only this time with an alternate version, one that we are more interested in.

So, we have answered the call and received the email successfully. Take a few minutes to process the information until it completely soaks in. Once you have understood the instructions, let us begin **the most important** phase of the interview.

It is nothing but an unfortunate fact that the majority of people tend to overlook this all-important aspect, thinking that they have all the 'knowledge' and 'experience' that merits them an opportunity. The interview is far more than just a brief look at the resume and the skills/experience section. You need to sell yourself, and if you do not know how to, then no employer on earth will hire you.

Knowing is half the battle won!

It is indeed the case. If you prepare well enough, you have already conquered half the phase well before the actual interview itself. Come to think of it, this does instill a sense of confidence and achievement within us, and it is that confidence that will take us through the other half of the journey.

To begin with, take some time out and start searching for information about the firm, even if you may know what the firm is all about and what it deals in. You will need all the knowledge you can gather because the employer might ask you if you have any idea what the company does. You can answer no, but that is not encouraged as it would show that you are not prepared to handle situations and might need a little training. If the position is marked urgent, they will prefer someone who already knows what needs to be done over hiring someone who needs to be taught first.

Get started on Google, or any other search engine of your choice, and find out about what the company does. Check out all the products and services. You do not need to memorize their pricing, budget, market position, or any of that. What you need to do here is to familiarize yourself with what the firm does and offers to the community in general. This is where you will start seeing how your particular set of skills or academic qualifications might come in handy.

In an ideal world, you would start taking some pointers and connect the dots. If the company is known for providing services where sales skills are required, brush up on your sales skills. If you do not have prior sales experience, browse through videos and tutorials to gain some valuable insight into the world of sales. Having a vague idea about a task is always better than having no idea at all. You do not wish to be caught in a question where you grow nervous and lose your composed state.

Once you have a fair idea of what the company in question does, it is time to move on to the next step. For this, create a checklist for your documents, academic certificates, degrees, transcripts, previous experience letters, and so on. It is best to carry out the exercise now and organize yourself beforehand rather than delaying the work for the 11th hour. That is something you should always avoid. Last-minute checkups are perfect if you have already taken the necessary steps earlier on. They turn into a nightmare if you begin at that very moment when you are just an hour or so away from the interview.

You might think, "I know what I need to take. My pictures, my ID, my documents, my resume; I don't need to worry!" Upon arriving at the venue, you realize you actually forgot to bring your previous experience letter. Imagine the nightmare that would immediately cause for you.

Ensure that you gather all the documents and keep them categorized in a neat folder that you can carry to the interview when the time comes. It always creates the impression that you came prepared. Going empty-handed will most likely see you walking out the same way.

Moving Forward

Coming up in the next chapter, we will start our journey into the "interview answers" and see just what kind of questions we can expect and what exactly we need to do to hit the mark every single time. However, before we do proceed, grab a handy audio/video recorder. If you wish, you can use your cell phone to start recording your answers for reviewing purposes. Our objective is to learn a few things when it comes to speaking:

- Our **volume** – There is a fine line between being energetic and downright loud. The latter is neither required nor appreciated.
- ***The tone of voice*** that we use – We do not want to sound monotonous like we are reading off of a script word by word. Bring in that natural element and let the words flow with their appropriate tones. Your words should reflect the energy and intentions. If you have been asked to explain something, and you do not remember or know the answer, using an excited tone to say "I don't know" will put any interviewer in a puzzled state.
- ***The speed*** at which we talk – If you are someone who rushes through words, you might end up in a spot of trouble. To you, you may have spoken perfectly well; however, the interviewer may have missed out on a word or two while trying to catch up. Use a pace that is both acceptable and understandable by anyone.
- ***Clarity*** of words – Pronounce every word clearly and correctly. Don't eat your words or mumble them just to cut corners and save time. This badly affects you and your candidacy.
- Your ***fluency*** matters a lot – Needless to say, too many 'Ah!' and 'Umm' will tarnish our chances of making it through the interview. What would normally take a minute to answer will now be prolonged to three minutes. Employers have neither the time nor the interest to listen

to everything you have to say. You need to keep everything crisp and concise and pay close attention to your fluency. Learn the words where you might feel your fluency breaks. Replace those words, where possible, to improve your fluency.

This is applicable to all the answers that you will learn in this book and any others that you may come up with on your own. This simple habit of recording your own voice and reviewing it allows you to essentially learn where you falter and find out techniques to improve your quality of answers and the delivery. The exercise takes a little time, but the results will be quick, and you will feel the difference yourself right away.

Now, we have pretty much covered all the prerequisites; it is time to move on and jump into the real reason that compelled you to buy this book: the successful "interview answers" to ensure your success!

Chapter 2: Facing the Popular Questions

In the previous chapter, we learned that there are quite a few things we need to research and practice to give ourselves a slight advantage in the interview. We went through the company profile, we established a basic understanding of what the company does, and then we found ourselves in front of the mirror, speaking to our reflection to see how effective we are as communicators. Now the time has come for us to begin unlocking the answers to some of the most common questions interviewers can and will ask you.

Depending on how well you answer these questions, you may either end up creating a perfect impression and securing the top spot or be one of those resumes that ends up in the trash can. The choice is quite literally yours. With that said, let us dive into these questions and see how **a student with no prior experience** would answer these questions. We will look at several questions and examples. Keep an eye out for some answers where you would be required to judge whether the answer merits a chance or if it deserves to be rejected.

Questions That Apply to All

Question: "Tell me a bit about yourself."

This is, without a shadow of a doubt, one of the most common questions asked by hundreds of thousands of interviewers and recruitment managers across the globe. Whether you are set to appear in person at a physical location or undergo your interview online, expect this question to come your way.

Before we begin, it is vital to try and understand why this question is so favored by many. This is one of those perfect ways to begin a conversation between a potential employer and a potential employee. Without wasting much time, this question basically asks you to highlight your background, including your current/previous experiences and academic achievements thus far. Naturally, this is where you either gain interest or lose it altogether. How? Let's have a look at the example answer below and see if the person merits an opportunity.

Answer: "Well, my name is Steven. My friends call me Steve. I am 28 years old, living at (some address). I love watching TV, and I absolutely adore 'Game of Thrones', Sherlock, and Marvel movies. I play baseball on the weekends. I got my master's back in 2007, from a well-known university.

I, uhh, love socializing and making great new friends. And I guess that would be it."

Yay or nay? If you chose the latter, you wouldn't be wrong. Fine, the TV shows this person mentioned were actually brilliant, but that is completely irrelevant at this point. This is a professional interview and hence does not require anyone to provide such information. If anything, the candidate failed to make an impression.

The employer is always short on time. They do not ask you such questions to know what your friends call you, which shows you prefer, what sports you play, etc. While the length of the answer might be acceptable, the content itself, minus the qualification part, was unnecessary. The resume is right before the employer, and the employer can already see your name. There was no reason why you should repeat that. Some might take that as an insult as well. You do not wish to cause a scene by delivering an answer where the other person, especially an employer, feels as if you doubt their credibility at reading.

Now, here's a more docile and acceptable version. Have a look and be a judge yourself.

Answer: "I am currently working as an assistant manager for a reputed firm. I was recently promoted to this position due to my dedication and effective team leadership skills that have certainly helped my managers and seniors save time and have someone they trust to take over matters that I can resolve. I do understand that your esteemed firm is looking for a person who can play that all-important role and assist the management in ensuring complete compliance while driving the team to work effectively as a unit to meet deadlines and achieve optimum outputs. For the last few years, I have helped organize team activities and training programs and ensured maximum productivity for the company and the team itself."

The person above immediately took a flying start by highlighting the selling points and strengths. He/she then provided the employer with an idea that this candidate has done a fair bit of research to understand the role and is ready to bring to the table all that is required by the company. Automatically, this answer will shine brighter for the employer, compelling him/her to move forward with the next question.

Before we proceed, try and analyze what makes this answer a good one. Sure enough, the employer has the resume and could've gone through these achievements and skills on his own. What the candidate did here was to take away the guessing game and bring the best forward. The answer is a perfect way to get started. But what if you are a student and have never had any previous job experience? How should you proceed?

Sure enough, you can always lie your way out, but remember this: What you lie about today will come back to haunt you tomorrow. Do not fall for the obvious "it's okay to lie in an interview" statement. Things have changed and it is now easier than ever before to verify credentials and claims. Stick to the truth here.

Student's answer: "I find myself to be a person with a great interest in developing my understanding and applying the knowledge I have acquired from my (bachelor's/master's) degree in practical settings. Your esteemed organization is currently looking for someone who is passionate to learn, gain experience, and possibly pursue a promising career in the field, and I believe I bring all of these components with me to the table to ensure I always go above and beyond expectations. Pursuing a career is a dream, but making it a successful one is what I tend to achieve."

Passionate, determined, and driven. The answer had quite a lot going on there. Sure enough, there were no lies at all, and the intention was clearly explained as well. However, you might wish to modify the answer to trim it down a little bit. The more you speak, the more boring it gets. There is also a risk that you might have just started to answer a question that could be your next. That happens a lot more than you might imagine. In the above, all seems to be fine except for a tiny detail. Look at the next question and try to understand what should have been omitted from this answer.

Question: "How would you describe yourself as a person?"

Immediately, you should be able to see that the part where the candidate described his/her qualities was meant to be answered now. Imagine how difficult it would be to find out you answered a question already and now you have to come up with another variant, all within a fraction of a second. Most likely, you would not be able to speak immediately and would be stuck with the annoying 'ahh' and 'umm' which would essentially seal the case, and you would have to restart your efforts all over again by searching for another opening.

Your answers need to be concise and to the point so that you only explain what is requested. There is no need to add unnecessary information unless the question specifically demands you to do so. Adding additional information is theoretically barring you from chances in the future to explain yourself clearly. Should another question pop-up where you are asked to define something that you have already been through, you cannot just go on and say, "Well, Sir/Ma'am, I have already answered that."

That would mean you are directing the interviewer instead of being directed by one. No interviewer will take that answer kindly. While they may maintain their calm composure and keep a friendly smile, rest assured you have blown your chances for good. The minute you walk out of the door, your resume is going to meet its fate in the bin.

To get into good practice, start by jotting down skills and traits you truly possess and excel at. Do not make things up as you go nor act like you know something if you have no idea what it may be. It is best to confess right away that you do not know it; however, add in a line to show that you are willing to learn.

Question: "Have you ever worked on Salesforce before?"

"Unfortunately, no, sir. However, I do not see that as a problem as I am a fast learner. With the right guidance, I should be up and running in no time."

This is just to demonstrate an example. The above might normally be asked if the job requires you to work with specific software or customer relationship management technologies like Salesforce. You will never encounter this question for any non-technical job.

Now comes yet another question that is quite possibly being prepared for you right this instant. It is best to put your thinking cap on and come up with a convincing answer to carry the interest forward.

Question: "Why do you wish to leave your current job?"

Okay, this is a tough question. Remember, the easier they look, the tougher they actually are. This question is carefully selected for people who have some previous experience and are currently working for another firm. The employer/interviewer has every right to know the answer to this question. How you answer it decides your fate within this company.

Here are three various answers. Consider this as a test for yourself and try to put yourself in the boots of an employer to gauge which answer merits your attention and which pushes your interest away.

Answer (i): "I am quite happy where I work; however, the pay that I have been receiving is far less compared to the kind of work I am asked to do on a daily basis. The market-competitive salary for such a job is (something), and it is only fair that I get decent pay at the end of the month to keep my motivation growing strong."

Answer (ii): "The company is a mess. There is no professionalism, and no one seems to care what you do or how you do it. There is chaos, the manager shows up when, and if, he wishes to arrive at work, the salaries are delayed, and the work is just never-ending."

Answer (iii): "I just believe that the time has come for me to seek a new opportunity where I can further enhance my experience and hopefully have better future opportunities come my way."

Which of these three do you think deserves the attention and which two deserve the door? Remember, you are now analyzing these answers as an employer. Take everything into account and come up with a decision. Once done, let us proceed and start by taking the answers apart, section by section, to better understand them.

In the first example, we see that the candidate has expressed satisfaction regarding the job and the workplace and has categorically stated the reason. He has further given statistics to support his claim regarding a low income and how it would boost his motivation to work. While there is a gray area in the answer regarding the kind of job he performs, the rest is absolutely acceptable and poses no eye-brow raising points.

In the second example, the candidate has wasted little time to show his displeasure over the state of affairs within the office. This is a situation that alerts the employer and the interviewer immediately. Badmouthing companies and workplaces is not only unethical, but it can, at times, even be illegal. If a candidate is revealing internal matters to another rival company, he/she may very well be in breach of certain terms and conditions pertaining to confidentiality. Take heed and avoid this path by all means. Not only would you be in line for rejection, but you might very well be facing a lawsuit coming your way should the word spread.

The third example is where things are a little tricky. This can go either way. Why? The candidate has expressed a willingness to enhance experience and knowledge, which is always a good sign. However, moving from the previous company to another just for the sake of pursuing something 'better' will probably create an impression that the candidate would not think twice about jumping ship in the future as well. This shows a lack of consistency and dedication to the company. A wise employer would only seek out talent and candidates who can stay as a part of the firm for longer periods of time.

The takeaway here is to avoid anything that is either too direct in terms of complaints or vague in nature, as we saw in the third example. Stick to the facts and present yourself as a person who is willing to adapt and learn to perform better. Needless to say, your body language and the winning smile will add to the moment and provide you with the much-needed 'oomph' you need to create that impeccable impression.

Strengths and Weaknesses

This is applicable to every single individual, male or female, new or seasoned, technical or non-technical. The technical professionals have a slight edge as it gets easier for them to explain things; however, with a little modification to the answer, you should be able to answer questions related to strengths and weaknesses. All it takes is ensuring you do your homework.

Question: "What would you say are your greatest strengths?"

The question is an invitation. This is where you sell yourself to the employer and explain just what you have that others do not. Be descriptive and define your strengths with relatable examples where possible. Convince your interviewer that you certainly hold an edge over others.

Begin practicing by writing down your skills. If you are good with computers, write it down. If you can find something more specific like being exceptional at Microsoft Office, web browsing, network administration, or email handling, be sure to keep that within the answer as well. Again, this applies to almost all as these applications, and the software does not necessarily require any specialized learning.

You do not need to mention all the skills. Pick out the ones that are relevant to the job opening and explain how you can use these skills to improve your quality of work.

For our technical friends, such as software engineers, data scientists, and machine-learning experts, you can explain quite easily how well you know the programming languages, debugging, rendering applications, creating applications, training machines, etc. For any technical job opening, these answers would suffice.

With that said, let us look at an answer with an approach that can be modified for both technical and non-technical candidates.

Answer: "I have always found myself comfortable when it comes to handling data and emails. Owing to my effective accuracy and typing speed, I find it rather easy to handle a large volume of tasks with minimum error margins. I have been known to be a problem-solver as well. There is no greater accomplishment than to observe, understand, and then solve a problem using my mathematical skills, combined with my knowledge of Microsoft Excel. The job requires someone to have a firm command on both, and I am happy to report that I can deliver exactly that."

No rocket science there. You have only explained what you needed to. You have hit the bullseye and not wasted time explaining other skills that were not yet requested. You may certainly be tempted to shed a little more light on your other set of skills; try and avoid that temptation. That might very well be your next question.

It is mandatory for you to look at and establish what your skills are before you go to the interview. If needed, practice them a little since you may be asked to solve problems for demo purposes as well. While this is rare, it is still a possibility, and one that we cannot cover in this book but can certainly recommend.

Strength questions are designed to find out if you have the capability to self-analyze and bring out a skill set that is unique and in demand by the employers. If you keep your answer quite generic, you might not be any different from the person who left just before you or the one who will come after you.

Instead of stating that you know how to use Microsoft Office, highlight that you know how to use that and "especially Word/Excel/PowerPoint" to further add weight to your claim. Keep things interesting for you and the employer. The remainder of the conversation might be a lot more pleasant than you think.

Failing to answer a strength question can get you into some hot water. Be sure to know what your strengths are and allow yourself to be in a comfortable position to explain them. The better your answer, the higher the chances of gaining success.

You can change, modify, or add certain pieces of information that may suit your situation better. If you are applying for a job at a law firm, use some words to describe your expertise in law. Similarly, if you are applying for a call center supervisor, provide examples of how well you have led your team in the past, etc.

Let's move on to questions that will, in one way or the other, ask you to identify your weaknesses. These questions do tend to pose a problem to quite a lot of candidates. Let us first look at the question in the example below:

Question: "What would you say is your weakness, and why?"

The question seems fairly straightforward. Surprisingly, quite a lot of candidates end up answering within the lines of having no weaknesses at all or stating that they have yet to discover one.

We, as human beings, know that no one is perfect. The sooner we accept this fact, the better it will be for us. The day you start thinking you have no weaknesses or know everything is the day your learning curve will turn into a flat line. The employer is expecting you to answer with honesty. Sure enough, you are scared to do so because you think the answer might mean an end to your interview and possibly your chances for the said position.

Here's an answer where a candidate reveals a weakness and how he/she tends to overcome that:

Answer: "I do find myself as a person who finds it hard to say 'no.' There was a time when I would say yes to everything thing that came my way. Eventually, I was bombarded with work stress. Since these tasks were time-constrained, I had to rely on management tools to ensure I could deliver the work. Sure enough, the quality was affected, but it opened a new learning path for me. Now, even though I am not yet there, I would think twice before saying yes to ensure I do not commit to something I know I cannot deliver on time."

If you have weaknesses like time management, workload management, setting priorities, or missing out on certain technical knowledge, most of these are okay to mention and confess. On the contrary, if you have a short temper, you might wish to first train yourself to endure more. If you share this piece of information, you might not get a welcoming response from the other party. No one wishes to hire someone who is ready to tear things apart and create a chaotic situation.

Let's take a look at another answer to get a better idea of how you can answer this question more convincingly.

Answer: "There is a fine line between working hard and working smart. I have just come to realize that. Earlier, I was fixated on ensuring I put in maximum hours, but that was neither productive nor optimum. Now, I am learning ways to better manage my time and get things done within a shorter span of time, without compromising the quality."

Quite a way to put things forward. This answer allows the interviewer to know that the candidate is both hard-working and dedicated. It also leaves room to suggest that the candidate is willing to learn better ways of learning and working. Every employer would love to have someone with those qualities on the team working for them and benefiting the company itself.

Remember, you will need to answer these questions both carefully and confidently. It is okay to have a flaw, and it is even better to confess and take steps to correct it. Your potential employer will normally take the answer kindly unless you tell them your weakness is a pivotal component for the job. If that is the case, there is every likelihood that someone else will walk away with the opportunity.

Questions pertaining to strengths and weaknesses are designed to catch a candidate off-guard and make them reveal what they are trying to hide. If your answer sounds too good to be true, the interviewer will reject you right away. They are neither interested in taking a chance nor do they have the luxury of time to verify your traits and skills individually.

To prepare yourself perfectly for these questions, take a piece of paper and list your strengths on one side and weaknesses on the other. Start by matching these with the job description provided by the employer to see which of these are required and whether those are your strengths or weaknesses. This will take away the guessing game and will make you focus on answering both aspects. Revisit the answers as mentioned above and come up with your own version of the answers, if needed, to make it a little more personalized. Remember, you will always find confidence when giving a personalized answer compared to one that you may have read on the internet.

Chapter 3: Tackling Queries on Education

One of the most important aspects of any job interview is the part where you are asked to share details of your academic achievements. Quite a lot of people take it for granted that their master's degree or their post-doctorate degree will see them through the interview, only to be met with sheer disappointment and a rejection from the employer.

Just because you have some of the finest grades does not mean nor guarantee that you will end up with a job or that employers will be interested to offer you the job. We have seen it in the big movies that as soon as you acquire a degree, employers from across the globe are flooding your inbox with job offers. Do not expect that to happen here. Instead, work on your personality, your charisma, and that winning attitude. These are the key components to help you shine, regardless of the degree that you may have.

Your academic details are mostly just formalities. You are asked to tell what you may have done, and then you eventually submit a copy of your credentials for verification purposes. Once that is sorted, rest assured, there is a 90% probability that those documents will never be looked upon again by the employer. All that will matter now will be your skills.

If that is the case, why do they ask for credentials, to begin with?

Degrees are the finest way to ensure that the candidate has the necessary knowledge, or at least most of it, that is required in order to be eligible to work in said industry. If you are applying for a job as a software developer, you need some diplomas or degrees to assure your employer that you have the proper training and have the relevant knowledge to get you going. Without these, the employer may never consider hiring you, period! That, then, makes it quite important to understand how to tackle questions and present your answer to the interviewer. Let us begin by looking at how **not** to answer the question first.

Question: "What was your last qualification?"

Surely, this is a straightforward question. However, once you answer this, the next one might be a little tricky to answer.

Question: "Why did you choose this field of study?"

Were you forced to choose this field? Did you have an interest in this field? Was it that you were interested in doing something else but ended up doing this? There will be quite a few questions you will need to ask yourself first, and that is absolutely okay to do now. Once you are at the interview, you will not have much time. If you stay quiet a little longer than needed, the employer will know he/she touched a nerve, and that is never a good sign.

Always stick to an answer that pretty much says this:

Answer: "It took some time for me to discover where my interest was. After much deliberation, I found this field to be something that genuinely caught my attention and inspired me to pursue a career in it. I find myself quite comfortable with the idea of doing (field related) job and having a successful career in the future."

This reassures the employers that you are indeed a candidate with a passion for doing the kind of job they have to offer. Mind you, if your degree is in computer science (software and technology, in other words), and you are applying for a customer service job, the answer will need to be modified. There is no correlation between software and technology with inbound sales or customer services.

The employer would only be asking you this question as a formality and would probably not even pay attention to what you might have to say.

Indirect Questions

Oh! You are going to get a lot of those coming your way. Infamous questions range from questions like "Do you wish to ask any questions?" to "Why do you think you are suited for this job?" You will need to be fully prepared for these. These are commonly asked questions, and there is a high probability that you might end up being asked them. No worries though, we are here to see this through!

There are certain questions that may seem direct at first. It is only after a little thought that you realize there are several layers for you to cover. It is vital for you to learn some of these questions early on and practice. The employer will not always ask you to provide some examples pertaining to your education directly. You will need to keep an eye out for such questions and answer them accordingly.

The first question is simple. The answer is always yes, you have questions and then you ask them! Why? Well, it shows you are interested in the job and did your research well enough to be able to ask questions. But what about the second one? Let's focus on that one since it's often more difficult to answer.

When an employer asks you such a question, they are directly asking you to provide reasons. There is a part of this question that is both open and slightly indirect in nature. You will first need to cover the direct bases, meaning that you will need to sell yourself by providing a list of skills that you possess that can help you stand out from the rest. As for the indirect part, throw in a little information about your education as well. Explain that while others may have a degree or a diploma, you have a better one, owing to the grades or the level of degree (masters or Ph.D.) and the experience that goes with those. It truly adds value to your answer and provides the employer with something to consider.

Beware though, you might even be asked yet another indirect question. Before we look into the question and possible answer, imagine this scenario.

- You are applying for a job that usually requires a two-year associate degree.
- You have a master's degree in a similar field.

The employer already knows this and might ask you the following question to catch you off-guard.

Question: "Are you overqualified for this job?"

It may hit you and make you go numb for a second. It also sounds slightly uncomfortable as most might think that this question essentially ends their hopeful run for the opportunity. There is nothing to be alarmed about. If anything, you can use that effectively to your own advantage. How? Let us look at a possible version of an answer to this question.

Answer: "While it may sound like that, I believe that having a higher degree allows me to bring a higher level of expertise for everyone. It also allows me to lead by example and apply the higher knowledge to further enhance the output. My degree, I believe, will allow me to explore future possibilities within this firm, as well, where I can further increase my exposure and improve the skills I have developed so far."

The answer immediately sets precedence. You have effectively informed the employer that you are a positive thinker, that, to you, the glass is half-full. You have also assured your employer that you wish to 'lead' by an example and allow others to learn greatly from you. For any employer, that is a golden opportunity. No sane employer would be willing to pass this on.

Learn how to use your skills and knowledge to your advantage. The employer wishes to know if you have what it takes to work. With the proper degree/diploma, and a passion for work, it is your job to provide your employer with ample reasons why he/she should consider you over others. Using such answers, you are doing exactly that.

How to Handle a Question on Possible Gap Year(s)

You have solid work experience in your curriculum vitae. Everything seems perfect, right till the point where two years ago, you stopped working. Even before you may be called, someone has circled those gaps out for the interviewer to see and ask you about. Be ready to answer those questions with confidence.

Questions: "You have a two-year gap in your experience. Why is that?"

Answer: "After my last working year, I decided it was high time for me to pursue a higher degree. My ultimate aim was to acquire my master's degree from a reputable institution as it would then allow me to seek out better opportunities. It was something I could afford to do, and I knew it would help me get noticed."

It seems good enough; however, your interviewer is holding your CV and is able to cross-check these facts. If you used this answer and the last degree claimed on the paper is older, you will be in a world of trouble. Instead, remain honest. If you stopped working to pursue education, you can explain that you may have just sat for the examinations and are awaiting your final results. Alternatively, you can provide them with your own version of the answer, as long as it is true and verifiable. Avoid answers based on lies or ones showing that you were just too lazy to work. You do not want to create the impression that you are someone who would quit the job halfway just because you didn't feel like working anymore. Assure the interviewer that you did what you did only to come out better.

Questions pertaining to education, direct or indirect, are normally few in number. They are easy to answer and can be tackled by almost anyone. All you need to ensure your success is a bit of faith in yourself and your word and confidence to support the same. After some practice, it will be a walk in the park.

While there is absolutely nothing to worry about these questions, there is, however, a certain way to ensure you answer confidently, and that is to analyze the question properly and then answer it accordingly.

Here's a little exercise: Try and create five various answers for the question below. Record audio of yourself and replay each to see which fits the question best. Not only is this a healthy exercise to further polish your communication skills, but it is also an effective way to memorize answers and gain the capability to modify matters as you go along.

Question: "What makes you a unique candidate?"

Remember, direct and indirect scenarios are at play here; therefore, the answer must be appropriate.

With that sorted, let us move on to a difficult phase of the interview and get a taste of how hard it can be to answer some of these questions.

Chapter 4: Keep It Professional

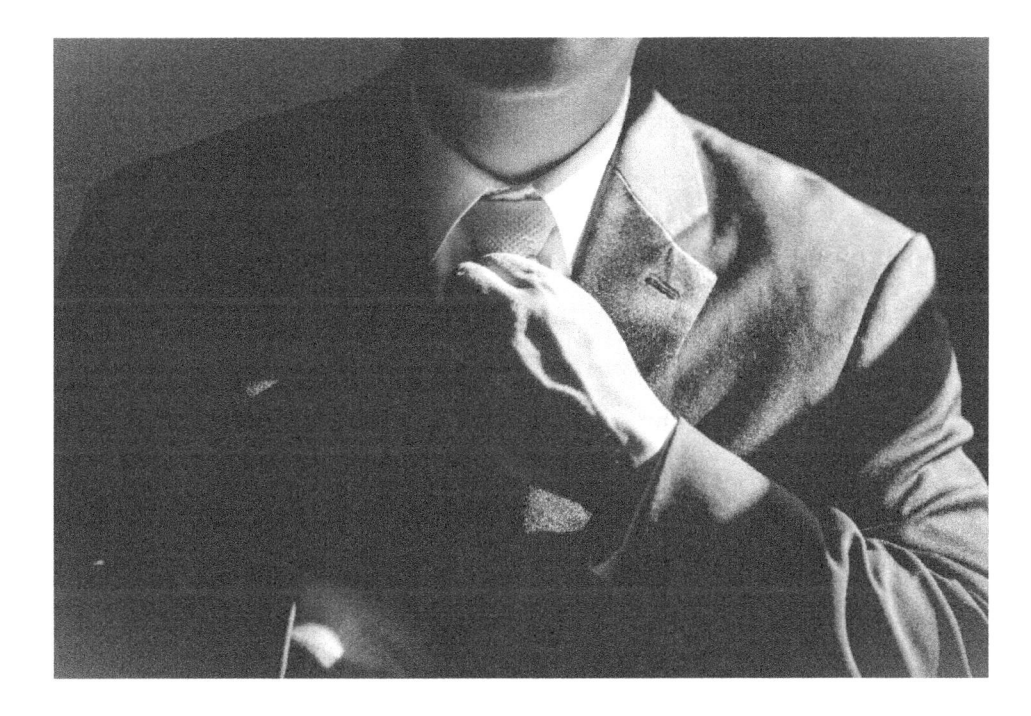

So far, you have been practicing a few basic, common questions. Now, things are about to change quite a lot. This is where the interviewer will be done asking you about you and your academic qualifications and achievements. You may have made a terrific first impression. Pat yourself on the back if you actually practiced a little. But now, it is time to shift into the higher gears and get our feet wet in the region where even the classiest of the first impressions can be decimated, destroyed, and shattered. All it takes is one wrong answer to make it all go 'Poof!'

This chapter will cover quite a few questions, all related to how you will need to answer questions regarding your previous experiences as a professional and your professional background as well. We will look into situations where you may be tested by certain questions to establish the kind of nature you possess as a professional.

For students who may have never had professional experience before, take notes. Draw inspiration from these answers, take notes from the ones you find relatable, and practice as much as you can, not as much as you like.

Describing professional experiences can be tricky, especially if you had numerous jobs over the past few years. There are quite a few things your employer will be looking for. Some of these are qualities while others fall under the category of risk assessment. Too much job-hopping and you may not make it to the finals unless you can come up with an extremely promising answer. As discussed a few times already, no employer is looking to hire someone who may be a worthy asset, only to find out that they are quitting within a year. It serves them no purpose and would push them to restart the hiring process all over again.

Q&A Where Your Behavior Matters!

Previously, we went through a question where the employer asked why we were quitting our current job. We have already seen how to tackle such questions. There are other questions that are both direct and indirect in nature. Here are a few of these questions you may find.

Question 1: "Tell me all about your previous work experience."

Question 2: "What is your greatest accomplishment?"

Question 3: "Have you ever faced a difficult situation? How did you handle it?"

Question 4: "How do you work under pressure?"

Question 5: "How would you feel if you were to report to someone younger than you?"

These questions are not random at all. Some of these, like the first two, are rather direct. The remainder of them requires you to utilize your experience and answer them accordingly. Should you be a student and thinking, "I have no experience. What about me?" Don't worry! We haven't forgotten you. We will look to answer these as well for students and first-timers.

Before you answer any question, it is vital for you to fully come to terms with the question and understand why it is being asked. The better you understand the question, the better you can answer. You can refer to another volume of the book called "Interview Questions" where hundreds of questions are explained in detail. Right now, we are only interested in a basic idea.

Question: "Tell me all about your previous work experience."

While the question is straightforward, the chances of you facing this question are quite high. This question is not necessarily dependent on the fact that you have previous experience or not. The question will be posed to you regardless of your degree, age, gender, or ethnicity. This question's purpose is to quickly catch up with your credentials instead of going through the CV for details.

Answer (i): "Currently, I am working as a manager for (company name). I have received training and gathered numerous accolades along the way. I have been known to be very good at what I do. I have enjoyed working under various leaders and have had the honor to be under the guidance of some of these. I learned how to be an effective manager, and by applying the knowledge and experience I gained from multiple positions, I made my way to the post of a manager. Before I joined this company, I was working at another reputable firm named (second company's name) for several years under the capacity of (role)*."

*Do not include the last line if you have no previous experience apart from your current job.

The answer is quite straightforward as well. No rocket science involved here that you will need to work hard on. With that said, there are elements to consider here. If you hold experience in a similar field, be sure to highlight that first. There is no reason why you should follow exactly the same order. Highlight your roles where you have performed phenomenally well. Never mention a job that you have been fired from. It would only make things seemingly impossible for you to conquer.

The aim of any interview answer that you deliver is to provide your interviewer/employer with the best selling points and reasons to come to the conclusion that you are the best of the lot. Half of the preparation should go into creating this mindset and accepting that. Only once you believe you have all the ingredients, skills, and traits to be the best there is can you deliver equally convincing answers.

For the students who may have had some exposure through internships, here's how you are to answer when such a question is posed to you:

Answer (ii): "I have only recently completed my degree program. During my degree program, I did have the opportunity to take up some rather fascinating internships which helped me evolve my knowledge and interpersonal skills. I believe those opportunities have helped me a great deal to ensure success in an organization as prestigious as this and prove myself to be worthy of being a vital part of the organization. My previous experiences have taught me how to solve problems, ensure compliance with workplace policies, and gain insight on what needs to be done in order to get the job done both productively and efficiently."

Again, this answer applies to you if you have any internships under your name. Even one would do you fine since the employer is looking to have someone who seems promising and dedicated.

If you stutter, feel nervous, or stop talking altogether, you are effectively throwing your opportunity away. Speak freely and speak honestly. There is no reason to be intimidated. The person who is interviewing you is only doing so because they need people like you. Your job is simply to prove that you are the right fit for the company.

For students with no previous work experience or internships:

Answer (iii): "As fate would have it, I have just recently acquired my degrees, and I am looking forward to applying my strengths and improving any of my weaknesses by stepping into the practical world and exploring how I can contribute to a firm. I am passionate about learning better ways to improve my own knowledge and skill set. I am known for being dedicated and result-oriented, which I believe is exactly the kind of person you are looking for, per your advertisement. I do understand I may have to undergo a probationary period, but I am happily looking forward to proving my worth as a team player and eventually gaining the trust of my fellow co-workers, seniors, and the company itself."

We mentioned two key components here. Can you guess which ones? This is a perfect way to create the impression that the employer is looking for. Not only have you provided them with an honest answer, but you have also shown that your desire to work and garner success is an untapped potential that the employer can dig into and utilize. Sure enough, the first time will always be somewhat intimidating. Do not let the fear and tension in the air get to you. Remain calm and composed. The beauty is we aren't facing the interviewer right now, are we? We have all the time in the world to practice these answers thoroughly and gain the key components of confidence and self-trust to see ourselves through.

Question: "What is your greatest accomplishment?"

When the employers ask you what accomplishments you have achieved so far, or which you hail as your greatest achievement to date, do not mistake this as a sign that your employer has taken an interest in your profile. While you may have delivered the finest answers, it is wise never to grow over-confident and mess up the remainder of the answers. Remember, we are in a territory where we are no longer dealing with elementary questions. Get any of these wrong or lie about them and you are as good as rejected.

A perfect approach to begin would be to use the STAR method. This is especially useful for interviews and helps everyone out with answering similar questions.

- **Situation** – Define a situation that is somehow related to something you accomplished and the job you are applying for, if possible. Think of a project where things weren't going great, but you were able to somehow turn them around.
- **Task** – Explain the objective of your task. For example, maybe your team's sales were low, and you were assigned the task to ensure the sales tally rose up.
- **Action** – Think about the plan of action that was taken into consideration and applied. You may have changed your sales pitch, trained your juniors, or taken extra training to further enhance your skills.
- **Results** – Needless to say, this is where the output comes in.

We will look into a model answer, but here is a little exercise for you to try. Grab a pen and paper and using the STAR method, try and answer the question yourself. Once done, put the pen down and just compare yours to the answer below. This is not a competition but merely a guide. There is a good possibility you might have already written something better. If not, you will have every idea now.

The answer will certainly have variations. The following is just a generic example. Modify the answer per your field of work, if and when required, to give it a more natural feel. Always try and personalize the answers.

Answer: "Not so long ago, my team members and I were assigned a task to ensure completion of research. While most thought it would be easier to work together on the project collectively, I knew there was room for a better approach. Therefore, I broke the project down into separate segments and assigned each member two segments. We were able to effectively focus on our sections and ensure the submission of the project well before the due date."

The above answer is generic in nature. You can modify the project to whatever applies to you. What makes this answer appealing is the fact that you are providing your employer with more reasons to pick you over your potential competition. This answer shows that you have certain management skills and are able to take on demanding challenges and leading roles as well.

For students with or without internships, you can shape this answer without many worries as well. There is nothing that limits you; thus, you can explore various versions of the answers. It would be easier if you would start writing your answers down and then start practicing using those answers.

The more you practice, the more comfortable you will be in delivering these answers at the time of the interview. Quite a few people tend to take an interview lightly, and they are making a huge mistake. Once you are within the confined room, even the best may feel unnerved and under pressure. Confidence is your best friend, and it is only achieved through practice

Question: "Have you ever faced a difficult situation? How did you handle it?"

This, perhaps, is a question that may take you by surprise. The problem is that our minds will immediately be bombarded by thousands of hardships we have faced over the years, and choosing one immediately is not an easy task.

You will be facing such questions often in various interviews. Understand that it is the sole purpose of any interviewer to push you out of your comfort zone and try to create a sense of uneasiness. This is designed to test the mettle of the candidate and see how he/she would be able to cope with difficult situations and questions. Anyone who succumbs to the pressure will not likely win any management positions soon. They may still be able to garner some attention from the employer for positions under specific departments; however, we are not looking to limit ourselves to those roles alone.

For the best answer, start decluttering your thoughts. Knock out situations that are irrelevant or emotion-driven. Remove all situations that involve petty issues. If you are lost on possible ideas, one of the safest bets would be to recall situations where you had to rely on your management skills. This could be something pertaining to how you carefully planned your finances for a specific month or resolved a problem that no one seemed to understand. Thinking of management tasks might just leave you with a few ideas. Write those down and analyze them. As an example, let us look at the answer below.

Answer: "Throughout my life, I have been known to be a calm and composed person. There have been times where conflicts erupted, especially at work, and I had to face quite a lot of opposition, and at times, it did get challenging. Losing my patience or temper is neither productive nor desirable. I am proud that once I was able to handle such a situation at work with my boss. I knew my boss had taken a step that would end up harming the reputation of the company. When asked for feedback, I provided my honest opinion and was immediately met with quite a few frowns and agitation. Some views that followed would have easily sparked some tempers; however, being a professional, I maintained my composure and listened to everyone's view. Surprisingly, there was a thing or two I corrected about myself as well. I am happy to report that my former boss and the team were able to steer ourselves clear of the impending mess and actually found a better way to move forward."

Again, this is just a general answer. You can change the answer as you see fit without moving away from the objective of the answer itself. The answer should instill a realization that you are a candidate with certain skills and confidence and have a vast knowledge about matters. Using examples where conflict management, time management, and/or technical issues are discussed shows that you are not one to shy away from a challenge.

For students:

You can explain how you prepared for assignments, presentations, and any other activity that involved the use of time-management skills, group discussion, leadership roles, and/or problem-solving skills.

Tip: If you are unable to come up with something of your own, think of that one brilliant teacher or colleague who was able to do something remarkably good that required certain skills to be utilized. You can always draw some inspiration from there and shape an answer that portrays that.

For students, the biggest cause of worry is the sheer number of "what if" statements that they bombard themselves with.

"What if they ask me about my grades?"

"What if they ask me to write a program?"

"What if they assign me a task far too difficult to pull off?"

These are just misconceptions and are very unlikely to ever take place in an interview. All you need is some elementary knowledge about what the position is and what kind of a firm you are about to apply to for the job. That information alone is enough to get you through. These questions are designed to gauge how you would behave in a given situation. These are called behavioral questions, and the internet is awash with information for these questions.

Answer easily, comfortably, and with confidence. There is no reason to panic at all. Assure the interviewer that he/she is speaking to the ideal candidate.

Question: "How do you perform under pressure?"

In this case, we will be looking into the classic example of a customer service representative. For anyone who has worked in this arena, they will know that they need patience and must remain calm and composed, even when the customer refuses to speak politely. These are trying times for any person. Only the finest of the lot are able to withstand the pressure and perform without faltering from their duties or role.

Quite a lot of employers love asking this question, even if you aren't applying for a customer service job. Just the question alone is enough to put a little pause in your train of thought and force you to regroup again to come up with an answer. The obvious trap isn't what you say, it's how you say it and how much time it takes for you to come up with the answer.

This is one of those questions that should be answered in a fluent manner, hopefully with very little hesitation, at most. The longer you delay your answer, the more you are tarnishing the impression that you may have created thus far.

Here are a few answers. Your job is to rate each of them on a scale of one to five, where the higher the score, the better the answer is. See if you can spot the weaknesses or strengths of the answers here. Just for this example, we will not take into account any hesitation or stutters.

Answer (i): "Well, I am someone who will try and give my best to meet deadlines. I try to steer clear of these situations as I am afraid I may not be able to focus properly on work under pressure. I find myself least productive when I work under pressure."

Answer (ii): "I don't see any reason why I should not be able to perform under pressure. As long as I know what needs to be done, it will be done. Pressure does not change the way I work; therefore, I see no reason why pressure should affect my work standards or quality."

Answer (iii): "I work perfectly well under pressure."

Answer (iv): "I understand that this job requires me to be able to perform at my best under pressure. I have extensive patience, and I am working on ways to further manage my temper as well to ensure I can be a perfect fit for the job."

Answer (v): "If the pressure involves meeting deadlines, that should not be a big deal for me at all. I do not delay matters or postpone things until tomorrow that I can do today. If the pressure situation involves dealing with overtime, I am afraid I cannot commit to that as I have other priorities to attend to as well."

Five answers, each with merits and demerits. Who do you think you would shortlist here? Let us start eliminating the ones that hold the least merits.

The first answer is an honest one. The candidate has clarified that he/she is not able to handle situations with pressure and wishes to stay clear of such scenarios. Clearly, if someone isn't confident enough or willing enough to take on challenges, there is little hope of such a candidate making it to the finals. **Goodbye, number one!**

The second answer certainly seems like a winner, doesn't it? While there is a hint of a gray area within the answer, there is little to mark this candidate down for anything. The candidate clearly knows his way around and is willing to take on the challenge. **Good answer!**

The third one is far too optimistic to be real. If you end up providing such an answer, you might not be considered, even if you actually possess the skills to handle the pressure. Remember, we need to sell ourselves and our skills. This answer is **will not be considered as good**.

The fourth answer started off brilliantly. There is evidence to suggest that the candidate has done his/her homework regarding the job. However, this candidate just managed to shoot himself/herself in the foot by mentioning how they are working to enhance their temper management. No employer would risk hiring a person who is willingly admitting to having temper issues. **So close!**

Lastly, the final answer. Again, the answer was honest and the candidate is intent on delivering work on time but has turned down the option for overtime. This answer resides somewhere **near acceptable**. If the job requires no overtime, the candidate is in a comfort zone already. However, it always shows dedication to the employer if the candidate says they are willing to work overtime if necessary. This is something you may find normal during the holiday season, especially within call centers, retail outlets, and chains. If you are applying for those, you may wish to reconsider your answer.

To wrap it up, we have seen how various answers leave different impressions. If you were an employer, sure enough, you would be shortlisting answer number two. If you had to pick another one, you can surely pick out the fifth answer. The rest either have major issues or are just too ambitious to be true.

Apply the same to your own answers. Do not make your answers sound unrealistic or far too optimistic. There is no room for being overly optimistic, and there is a fine line that you should steer clear of when being honest. The minute you step over the line, your honesty will be the only thing standing between you and the potential job offer. Know what you need to share and only share the information that is relevant and encouraging. Being blunt or extremely straightforward is never going to get you anywhere.

Employees and potential candidates are expected to possess some flexibility. Ensure that you know where you can be flexible and feel free to highlight that. The employers always appreciate candidates who are willing to be flexible for the betterment of the team, the bosses, and the organization.

Question: "How would you feel if you were to report to someone younger than you?"

Okay. This is a question that is not exactly common, but it is one that is being asked to people who may be slightly older than the average age of the employees on a team you are about to be a part of. Employers take a great interest in knowing whether people are genuinely okay with being under the leadership of someone who is younger.

Considering the fact that there are quite a few institutions and organizations where younger professionals are taking over bigger roles, it is a possibility that you may end up being a part of a team led by an individual who is younger than you. Younger could mean just about anything. The age gap could be as marginal as one or two years or up to a mind-boggling 10 years or more. Adjusting in such a situation is certainly going to have its challenges for you.

No one wishes to be bossed around by anyone, especially someone who may be considerably younger. However, as professionals, we need to blur the lines a little and develop our tolerance and accept the facts. Should you provide a hint of doubt within your answer, you may not make it through your interview.

Answer: "It is perfectly understandable if I am to work under the leadership of a professional who may be younger than me. I do not hold any doubts in my mind nor complaints if that is the case. I am here to perform my duties as an individual and as a team player, and hopefully, one day, I will prove my worth to be standing next to such professionals as equals by learning from their guidance."

Ambition is good as long as it sounds realistic. This answer does not provide any room for overflowing optimism or an ambitious nature. The candidate composed an answer that is not only acceptable but also appreciable in nature. Our aim is to ensure we can provide the same answer when such situations are met. There is every possibility that at least one department of a firm is being looked after by someone who is younger than we are, unless we stand at the minimum age ourselves. The quicker we show acceptance of the fact that we may end up reporting to someone who is younger than us, the better it will be for us and the employer. How you deal with the professional once you are hired is something that falls outside the scope of this book, and hence, will not be covered here.

The Big Takeaway!

In this chapter, we came across quite a few answers to some of the most challenging questions that are quite common, if not the most common ones. Depending on the kind of job you are applying for, you may wish to modify the answers accordingly.

All the answers shared within this chapter were mostly generic to ensure greater ease of changing or modifying them as you see fit. The answers will remain acceptable as long as you do not end up adding something that opposes the question or any values.

Ensure that all your answers are delivered clearly, and one way to ensure that is through practice. We can't urge you enough to practice as much as you can. By now, you should have already practiced a few answers. Add a positive and energetic tone, bring in body language and gestures as well, and you will eventually be able to master the art of communication.

While that will cover one aspect, the other aspect will be the content of the answer itself. Be sure to provide reasonable clarifications, where possible. Do not leave any gray areas for employers to exploit. Our first order of the day is to ensure we provide all the knowledge and cover all the bases properly. Doing that will ensure that the employer doesn't need to rely on 'guessing' what you may have meant when you delivered your answer with a hint of doubt or gray area.

Practice these five questions over and over again. Generally, you will only be facing one to two of these questions in an interview, apart from quite a few others. Consider this book as a little cheat sheet for you to get a head start. The more you practice, the more you will realize your mistakes. If you have been following the tips so far, you might have already been recording your voice and various answers as well. Try and see where you are using the perfect tone of voice, where you are stuttering, where you may be faltering, and where you may need to improve.

Right now, you have all the time you need to figure out these errors and strengths. Once you are at the interview, you will be at the mercy of your own answers that only the employer will be able to gauge and mark. Do not let yourself be in a position where you cannot help yourself to achieve the job you are seeking. Master the art of answering questions confidently and comprehensively. Know which questions require a specific kind of information and which ones require you to answer briefly. Anything that falls out of the scope of the question should stay that way. Do not try and add unnecessary information or fill out the answer with made-up stories. There is a very good likelihood that what you may be making up as you go along, you might not remember just two questions further down. It is standard procedure to record the conversation these days, and you might have already spelled your doom if you made up a story and said something completely different a question or two later.

Remain composed and confident! You have all the answers in the world. All you need is the right way to put them. Practicing these answers and the ones that are to come in the next chapters will pave the way for you to achieve all the success you need.

Chapter 5: The 'Why' Question

If you thought the previous questions were tough enough, this chapter will cover the questions that will surely to stump you. These are notoriously infamous questions where the employer will directly ask you questions and might even hope to provoke some kind of reaction that would be evident within your tone or the change of it. There is no reason to take any of these questions personally. The interviewer is only doing what needs to be done to ensure only the finest of the lot is filtered out and set up for final interviews, if and when needed.

The questions in this chapter will revolve around the word 'why' where you will once again be needing to bring out that salesman within you to sell your skills, your charisma, and your experience/knowledge to the interviewer. By now, you should have already acquired a good idea on how to do that. Surely, we cannot expect you to answer all the questions within the first go, but that is exactly what we are trying to achieve by the end of this book. We want to be the people who will not waste any time and answer the questions right away.

Tip: *You can take a second or two before you begin to answer. Use that fraction of time to gather your thoughts. Do not jump into answering the question the second you think the question has ended. It will sound like you have revised a script, or you may end up interrupting the interviewer right in the middle of a question, thinking that the question actually ended.*

When you are asked a 'why' question, pay close attention. Ensure that you fully understand the question and what is needed of it. It is just like someone asking you why you use this cell phone over that. You will need to be ready to defend yourself and your interests. That can only be done if you know what you need to talk about. Remember, just because you may be experienced does not necessarily mean that you are better than your competitors. You need to bring a solid reply, an unshakable answer that merits attention from the employers.

Let us jump right into the answers by first looking at a question and seeing how we can tackle the question with an equally appropriate and compelling answer.

Question: "Why have you chosen to work here?"

If you are not slightly baffled by this question, then you are either confident enough to handle the situation on your own or you have just not realized the difficult nature of this question yet.

The obvious thought that may hit our head might not be the one we should lead with. In most cases, it would be owing to the fact that you are either unemployed or you have learned of a better opportunity within said firm. No one in their right mind would let go of an opportunity of earning a better income, right? The problem is that quite a few candidates actually end up using that as an answer. Sure, the money is the biggest motivation for any salaried person, but using money as your sole answer is neither professional nor recommended. It does create a rather distasteful impact. Here is a look at a few examples to see how such answers can ruin our efforts and create the kind of impression that pushes us back straight through the doors we came in from.

Answer (i): "I am unemployed at the moment. I could certainly use the money to pay my bills and meet my needs."

Answer (ii): "I have heard that the salary offered here was rather attractive. I would certainly love to be able to draw a higher salary compared to what I am currently drawing."

Answer (iii): "I can provide you a one-word answer to your question: money."

Let us be brutally honest here. Would we ever hire someone who is clearly driven by the desire for money alone?

These answers do look good in a TV series or a movie, but in real life, things work quite differently. Every employer and interviewer knows there are hundreds of candidates waiting outside in case you decide not to play your cards right.

Out of all the three answers, the second answer was somewhat acceptable, but the candidate was not able to cash in on the opportunity completely. There is no denying that higher pay attracts everyone, just as the second candidate said. This effectively places this, or any other candidate, into a risk assessment grid where these profiles will be marked as potential future risk, in terms of retainment.

Employers may view this answer as an early warning sign that the candidate, should he/she be selected, would not hesitate in shifting to another firm offering slightly higher pay scales. One way around the matter would be to bind an employee in a contract, but that would perhaps be frowned upon and, in some cases, illegal as well. To ensure the sustainability of work and productivity, employers and interviewers seek out profiles that show signs of dedication and promise.

With that said, let us modify the answer and see what a perfect answer to such a question would be. We will also include the money part, just for information's sake.

Answer: "The organization I work for currently is indeed a good starting place. However, I believe I am being under-utilized by doing repetitive work. Your firm has a reputation for being one of the leading names in the country. I have always wanted to be a part of an organization where merits are valued and employees are encouraged to do their best. I have done my fair share of research and learned that employees here are highly motivated by being recognized for their work; rewarded handsomely through bonuses, high salaries, and perks; and trained by the best. To me, that is more than any employee can dream of."

Yes, we did use a little flattery here, but there is no harm in that. The interviewer or the employer should feel like they are speaking to someone who praises the efforts and the working environment. It naturally prompts them to take a little more interest in your profile. Add that to an answer like the one we just saw above, and you have yourself a perfect scenario in the making. So, what exactly happened in this answer that made it sound so much better?

The answer began by highlighting that we are currently working at an organization or firm that is lacking a few core values. We then provided a little hint that we did our homework about this new place and its employees. Even if you haven't done that, you do not need to worry.

By sharing the information you gained on how happy and productive employees are here, you have informed your potential employer that you know what you are talking about. You kept money and bonuses as a secondary element, which further adds value to your answer because you are more concerned about being a productive worker who is praised and hopefully promoted over being paid higher. That does not mean that you are looking to work for free either. There is every indication that you hope to cash in on the opportunity yourself, but this way, your answer seems more promising.

Apart from this question, let us look at another 'why' question that often intimidates and breaks candidates into pieces. If there was one question from the entire interview that deserves the highest attention, it should be this one!

Question: "Why should we hire you?"

Phased already? We haven't even begun to look into the answer yet and already we feel slightly uneasy. As natural as it may be to feel that way, we need to ensure that it does not falter or shatter our confidence.

Take a deep breath, gather your thoughts, think through whatever you have said so far, and deliver the answer. As an exercise, try and attempt this question on your own.

Tip 1: *The answer should cover what, who, where, when, why, and how.*

Tip 2: *The 'who' in the answer is either you or your employer. Think the remainder through and compose your answer accordingly.*

If you really thought we would just skip past the toughest question, think again. We will now be looking at a possible answer that you can use at the time of the interview. Once again, modify the answer where and when possible to suit the situation better. Whatever you may have written, compare that with this and take notes where necessary.

Answer: "There are quite a few reasons why I believe that I am the perfect fit for this job, chief of all are my own personal values. Even though I have spent just a limited time within this organization, I can already sense that the organization's goals and my personal values align perfectly. Everyone who works here is working out of passion instead of need, and I truly believe in the concept that shows how one can achieve phenomenal success should they have a passion for it. I admire what this organization has done. If I am hired, I bring the desired passion, knowledge, and all of my skills to the table that would allow me to fit in immediately and further add to the success of the organization."

Now that was not as hard as you may have thought, right? The answer is rather self-explanatory. Remember, the question was never posed to intimidate you; it is only our mind that makes room for fear to creep in. There is nothing about any of the questions you may have already seen or might encounter ahead that should alarm you in any way. All you need is a clear mind and proactive listening skills to do half the work for you. The other half is how you compose your answer, identify your strengths, and present them to the interviewer. There is nothing in the world that can stop you from achieving success in any job interview that you may face in life.

Have a look at the tip we came across earlier. Remember the what, who, when, where, why, and how? Let's see how those were covered here.

What – That is perhaps the most obvious one. The 'what' here reflects on what we will be bringing to the organization in question, our skills!

Who – This would normally pertain to you, the candidate; the employer; or the organization.

Where – That would be the organization's physical location, a department, a team, etc.

When – The 'when' part was covered the moment we mentioned

"If I am hired…"

Why – This is where we covered the reasons itself using 'what' and 'where' mostly.

How – If you have not yet figured this out, do not worry. We covered the 'how' when we spoke of how passion and our skills would allow us to fit in and contribute to the goals of the organization.

Structure your answers similarly for all these questions. Ask yourself if you have covered these areas. If you feel like you forgot something, start all over again. Right now, you have all the time you like. Use it well, and use it productively. Prepare for answering these questions with ease and a clear approach. The more you falter, the easier it will be for the employer to bid you farewell.

Why This Role?

Let us assume that you have applied for a position as an assistant manager at a firm. You are slightly overqualified for the position, which may provide you with an edge and an equally difficult situation to handle, one that your employer would not shy away from asking about.

For the sake of a healthy debate, your employer has decided to change the topic and find out how you would fare in a role that is normally suited to someone who is less qualified than you. There is no reason to be alarmed here. The only reason your employer should be asking this is if he/she has spotted the obvious and wishes to ensure you are indeed okay with the idea of being in a position that is below your qualifications and experience. There are certain times in life where we may have to switch careers, and this might just be that.

We will be looking at two important questions here and some exceptional answers that can and should convince most of the interviewers easily, provided that you were able to begin on a proper note and continued giving your employer the perfect answers.

Question: "Why are you interested in this role?"

Once again, do not let the immediate thought be your eventual answer. Pause for a second and give it a thought. If you have done your homework and researched the job description and duties involved, you will fare far better in answering this perfectly.

Begin by highlighting how your particular set of skills is something that the company values and needs at the same time. You have already laid a solid foundation in the previous questions that have been asked so far. Use that to your advantage. Use phrases like "as I mentioned earlier" and "per the advertisement, the job requires (traits), and as it happens, I excel at these…"

To give you a better idea, here's an answer to the exact same question by our friend, the candidate.

Answer: "I believe my expertise, rich experience, and knowledge can greatly be highlighted through this role. As per the advertisement, all the duties involved are aspects I consider to be my strengths and areas where I can perform exceptionally well. While some may argue over the fact that I may be overqualified, I do believe that can actually benefit me and others around me to seek out more effective methods to see through a task and achieve the set goals and desired results with finesse and ease."

No fancy words, a balance of ambition, reality, and optimism—just what the doctor ordered.

While this answer may seem satisfying, the same can be applied for students as well. Just remove the phrase "rich experience" and you already have a perfect answer that is ready to be delivered. If you wish, you can certainly modify the last sentence to make it sound more acceptable. Sure enough, relying completely on that last sentence may get you a curveball coming your way. The employer might even ask how you can prove your skills since you have never worked before. An effective way to dodge the bullet would be to take a proactive approach and assure them that you know these tasks well owing to internships or university projects where you played your part and achieved the required results effectively.

Practice with all the variations to this answer and choose the one that you ultimately believe will get the job done. One fine way to tell if you are on the right track is to listen to your audio yourself and analyze your answer with all honesty.

Should you find a hint of doubt, room for improvement, or anything like that, revisit your answer and improve it as much as you can. You will need all the practice and confidence for the coming interview.

The Easier 'Why' Question

There is one situation that we have briefly touched upon in this chapter, yet we still have not seen a question pertaining to that. If you are someone who belongs to a different career path and has decided to change careers, for whatever reason, expect this coming at you.

Question: "Why are you changing careers?"

Truth be told, this question may look easy, but it is indeed a bit harder than you might expect. Coming up with a perfect answer for this is virtually impossible as each and every candidate may have a different reason why they may be inclined to make the change.

If you have been paying attention so far, we have already knocked out money as the reason. Sure enough, it is our aim to earn as much as we can, but our employers don't need to know that; at least, not right now. What else can you possibly think of then?

- Peer pressure?
- Better career advancements?
- Better perks?
- Easier working conditions?
- Flexible working hours?
- Newly found expertise?

Whatever your reason may be, you will need every possible and logical reason to help you deliver a promising answer. Hopefully, the answer will be one that does not leave you baffled before or after you deliver it.

Naturally, students are not expected to face this question but do take notes if you like.

We shall now look at a possible answer. This one concerns a former software engineer who has decided to pursue a career in graphic design instead.

Answer: "Since I was a child, I was always fascinated with artwork, painting, and creating designs. While I am a software engineer, and I get to use my creativity to come up with new software and applications, I believe that these do not do me justice. I am the kind of person who wishes to push my creativity and thinking abilities to the max, and graphic design is the field that would allow me to do so. Not only would I be doing something I am passionate about, but I would also be learning how to do it effectively and professionally through this job."

Needless to say, our dear friend here covered all the regions. The candidate skillfully provided reasons and showed an inclination toward art and designing. Take any part of the answer out and immediately, things become a little blurry.

Once again, you may notice that there is no evidence to suggest that the candidate is more interested in pay or showing any signs of job-hopping. There are virtually no points to fall under the risk assessment grid, unless previous experiences have shown a consistent nature of career switching. If that is the case, you best prepare your mind for a rejection. The world today has quite a lot of talent out there. If you fail to provide a justification for your profile and your own professional credibility, someone else will. As a result, that person will walk away with the employment contract as well.

To conclude this chapter, let us recall what we have seen and learned so far. This chapter focused primarily on the kind of questions that demand you to provide reasoning. These are the tough, tedious, and at times challenging questions starting with the much-feared 'why' word. Dealing with such questions is no ordinary task and deserves special treatment.

We looked at the first 'why' instance earlier on as well, but in this chapter, we dove into the deep end and figured out how to answer the following questions, just to name a few:

- Why have you chosen to work here?
- Why should we hire you?
- Why are you changing careers?

None of these questions are as easy to answer as they may seem. Each one of them revolves around your skills of maneuvering the discussion to where you want it to go. If you are trying to make a winning impression, you need quite a lot of practice and nerves of steel to remain calm and composed. Often caught off-guard, candidates end up shattering their confidence when faced with such questions.

There is nothing to be alarmed about. Every question that is posed has a reason. The employer only wishes to confirm that whatever you claim to have is verifiable and true in nature.

Think about it this way: If you were to hire a few people from over 100 applicants, what would you do? Whom would you hire? To fully understand and appreciate the significance of these questions, step into the shoes of the interviewer and then compose an answer that they would love to listen to. If you are able to pull that off, there is nothing in the world that is stopping you from ensuring a perfect closure.

These questions, hard or easy, need your attention and need to be understood correctly. This chapter showed a few variations of answers to prove just that. The answers also showed how we need to prioritize matters and how not to ruin or damage our first impression.

Put aside your greed for monetary gains and benefits and focus primarily on the long-term goals. Show the employers that you aim to stick by their side in the long run. There should be little to doubt about your answers and your credibility. Since you will have a limited time, it is vital that you practice these answers beforehand.

Tip: Create a small list of skills and rate them out of 10 to gauge your own self as a professional. Once you have your skills and merits marked, use only the top three strengths throughout the interview. You will normally be using two at most, but knowing which two or three to use before the interview will be a big help during the interview.

Practice by writing, reading, and saying your answers out loud. Analyze your own versions of the answer and compare them with the ones within this book. Hopefully, you should be able to come up with perfect answers on your own by now.

It is time for us to move into the part of the interview where we will discuss some more questions that are normally not frequent in nature. However, that does not mean that they are not important. If your interviewer asks you a question, you will need to ensure you provide an answer, even if that is 'no!'

Chapter 6: The Unusual Questions!

Interviews aren't always about testing someone's patience alone. Sometimes, you may encounter questions that are designed to see other things that are not categorically related to the job you pursue.

There are hundreds of such questions that you can find all over the internet and in YouTube videos, and tons of books cover these, as well. However, the fact of the matter is that they are not classified properly in most of these cases.

Here, the questions that are unusual but not necessarily uncommon have been provided for you under an appropriate heading. The answers we will go through in this chapter are to serve you as an added advantage over the bulk of knowledge you have already acquired by now. To make the most of the knowledge, browse different articles and videos to further fine-tune your responses in accordance to your profession.

If we are discussing an example regarding a software engineer and what his/her response would be, it may not completely apply to someone who is in a non-technical field. Instead of confusing yourself with rather vague and tough-looking terminologies, replace those with what applies to your profession. The best way to do so is to search online. There are hundreds of forums and social media websites such as Quora that will offer you expert advice on specific field related questions. This book is best to get a general idea of things and prepare yourself to answer any situation and question that is thrown at you.

Time has come for us to dive into rather unusual questions, and we truly mean unusual!

Sorry, What?

This is probably the reaction first-timers normally end up with when they are posed with one unusual but common question. How? Let us first set the tone right and create this virtual scenario for ourselves to completely understand the matter at hand.

You have applied for a job at a reputed firm. Fortunately, after much anticipation and sleepless nights, you get the magical email that begins with the word 'congratulations.' Sure, you are chuffed about it, and you take everything into account. You have all the necessary information you need about the job, you have all the documents, and best of all, you have the confidence to face all the tough questions.

You arrive at the venue for the interview, and you are eventually called in. After many questions, the employer seems to be keen on you. Just when you thought you had conquered everything, next comes a question that leaves you clueless.

Question: "What is your expected salary?"

Stunned? You have every right to be. After all, they are the interviewers and employers, shouldn't it be their job to let us know what we can expect instead of the other way around?

There is a science behind such a question. Without diving into the details, let's get straight to the point. This question is designed to see what you expect. If you quote a figure that is too high, you will lose your ground and raise a red flag that you might switch your workplace the minute someone else pays you more. If you say too low, they will not waste any second ensuring you are finalized, and they may not reveal that you could have gotten quite a lot more had you known the market-competitive salary. Both ways, you are at risk of either being rejected or being underpaid.

You will not be able to answer this at all unless you know exactly what you need to quote as an answer to this question. There are two ways you can do that.

1. You find someone you know who works within the office and ask them about the salary.
2. You use websites like https://www.indeed.com/salaries to find out the perfect market average.

While the chances of the first situation being true are somewhat good, your safest bet is the second source.

Using the online guide and finding out about the average pay scales will greatly help you prepare for this question. The answer is quite simple and involves fewer words than any of the answers we have come across so far.

Answer: "I am expecting a salary range of $65,000 to $70,000 per year. I have done my research and know that this is what a person of my experience/education normally gets."

Tip: *Should the survey say a range of $60,000 to $70,000, be sure to stick to the maximum figure or increase the lower side of the range considerably. We do not wish to settle for the bare minimum.*

This has been said over and over again, but every single time you deliver an answer, be sure to have the confidence to back it up. If you sound unsure, uncomfortable, or anything other than confident, the interviewer will take advantage of that.

Suppose you answered the above, and the interviewer said that it is somewhat higher than the job may pay "at the start." That is yet another way to get you to lower your expectations. This is the part where the ball is thrown in your court. Use it well and negotiate accordingly. Once again, do not fall below the market average. You can be honest and let them know it is not feasible for you to work for anything under that as it would not meet the expected budget and commitments that you may have.

It is always admired by employers when you are being flexible. With that said, do not be more flexible than needed. Some employers do have a reputation for exploiting workers and employees only on the grounds that they are extremely flexible. Ensure you know your minimum threshold and try your best to remain above that. If absolutely crucial, show some leniency. You may actually end up making a deal that would benefit you after all. If the employers are not ready to move an inch, it is best to understand that they will carry on causing more problems later on.

In some countries, it is normal to see job postings with a fixed salary mentioned. If that is the case, and this question comes up, you can reply accordingly as shown in the example below:

Answer: "If I recall, the advertisement stated that the job pays $65,000 per year. While it was mum on whether this is before or after taxes, I believe it is appropriate enough for me to begin with."

The answer remains plain and simple. It shows you are all set to join the company and carry out your duties accordingly.

In some cases, you might come across questions that are specifically related to the job you are applying for. They may not ask you to do or answer something that is technical, but they may ask you to explain what you think a specific job is all about. The question is slightly unusual because you may not have the experience, but that would only make things a little more difficult for you to answer.

Question: "What do you think customer service is?"

For anyone who has never worked in a customer service department before, you might be taken by surprise here. There is no reason why you should feel this way. You already know quite a lot about it. There have been movies, articles, books, and videos that you may have already gone through well before you applied for the job. Use that information, and you are still good to go.

Answer: "Customer services, as far as my opinion goes, are the backbone of any business organization. Whether you are selling physical/virtual products or rendering services, you need an exceptional customer service department to look after the customers and ensure they win their confidence every time the customer decides to call. It is one of the most effective ways to get immediate feedback from the customer as well. It also allows customers to get in touch with us and let us know if they are happy or face issues from using our products/services."

Once again, the candidate gave a general overview of things. There is nothing specific to worry about here; otherwise, you would be seeing names like Salesforce, CRMs, Ticketing Matters, and so on. Keep the approach general and explain in a way that even a layman would understand. Remember, the interviewer is most likely a part of a recruitment team. They may not have the same knowledge as you do, but the better you explain, the more they realize you are an effective communicator.

Moving on to our next entry, the one that gets everyone excited and serves as a mood changer. If you are expecting a question like when you can join, it is too soon to look into that for now. The question here is somewhat unusual and slightly uncommon as well.

Question: "What is your ideal job?"

Oh boy! We can write a mountain of pages on that, can't we? Here's a look at some of the answers you might imagine.

Answer (i): "Well, I would love to be a host at The Grand Tour."

Too brief and a little too ambitious. It is good to dream big, but this answer is not serving the purpose here.

Answer (ii): "I would have to say that I would love to be leading a firm of my own one day."

Nothing too ambitious, but there is a certain hint of risk that the candidate would leave once he/she has earned enough and is ready to begin their own separate venture. This could also raise red flags as the person would now be considered as a potential risk, since they may use internal information, client data, and any other operational methods to run their own operation.

Answer (iii): "I do not believe there has to be a specific job for it to be called an ideal job. I believe any job can be ideal as long as I have the willingness, dedication, and passion by my side."

Let's be honest. This does sound a little diplomatic, but it is one that is most likely to win out of the three answers here.

Answer (iv): "I am already here, being interviewed, and I consider half my dream fulfilled already. The other half depends whether I get this job or not. I truly am passionate about working in this organization and making my way to the top of the ranks through my skills, expertise, and knowledge."

The tone remains exactly like the one we saw in the third answer. The only difference is that this candidate has highlighted this specific job opportunity to be the one that they truly wish to take. Sure enough, this one is a winner as well.

Here's your exercise for this chapter. Come up with five various versions of what you believe would be an ideal job for you. Bring originality to the table and see what kind of tone and message they bring forth.

The purpose behind asking this question and knowing how to answer it is to let the employers know that you have certain skills that can be used at a later stage. These may include knowledge about software, hardware, IT, call handling, management, leadership qualities, really, the list could just stretch endlessly. Be sure to answer by providing something promising that the employers can remember at some point in the future. The better your answer, the more chances you create for yourself for promotions. Mind you, you haven't even been hired yet and already you are being considered from this day forward.

Keep an optimistic and original approach to matters. Do not be too concise on this question or provide more details than needed. Ensure that your answer is clear enough by providing a hint of what exactly you aim to do later on in life. Anything that goes against the company's interest, like parting ways and beginning your own venture, you should keep to yourself for now. There is no reason for your potential employers to know of that just yet. When the time is right, and you are established, you can then look into the idea of sharing this with your colleagues.

Questions for You to Practice!

Unusual questions come up every now and then. They are not as common as you might think, but it is wise to be ready for these as well. Before we move ahead with the next chapter, here are some questions for you to work on and practice. Come up with the best possible answers. If needed, take additional support from the internet, books, and articles. The more resources you have to rely on, the better your knowledge will be.

Questions:

- "If you could change something about yourself, what would it be?"
- "How many coins would you need in order to create a stack as high as the Empire State Building?"
- "Would you like to work in the morning or in the evening?"
- "If you had to choose one superpower, what would it be and why?"

Rest assured, most of these are questions that have been reported by various candidates on various platforms. These questions, as weird and unusual as they may sound, hold certain pieces that allow the interviewer to further dig in and analyze you as a professional. Our job is to ensure we practice only what we need to speak about. Speaking of things that might negate or oppose our own previous answers and views would end up creating confusion and might fetch a possible rejection as well.

Chapter 7: A Whole Bunch of Answers!

We have now arrived at a point where all the major questions have been covered. These so far did not include any brain-teasers or technical questions. If we were to dive into technicalities, we would end up with hundreds of books, if not thousands, just to cover all the possible jobs and questions pertaining specifically to them. What we can cover are a whole bunch of questions and their respective answers that may seem loosely related to the job.

These include questions that may ask you if you like watching a specific genre of movies or listening to songs while you are driving. These may be questions where you may be asked to define your greatest fear or phobia, or questions that are open-ended and quite literally allow you to be as imaginative and ambitious as possible.

There is no denying that every interview is different. Every candidate who has walked through the doors before you and will do so after you have left will face a set of various questions that are asked randomly. There is no specific order that is followed. You can only predict the situation and have a decent idea of what the interviewer might ask you next, but that is it; you can only predict.

This chapter will cover questions that neither you nor anyone else can predict, let alone expect them to appear in the first place. These are questions that will not serve much of a purpose. Their only job is to keep the interview alive and see if you are indeed comfortable in answering questions that you may never have expected to encounter.

These questions are your green light to go and deliver the finest answer you can think of. There is no wrong answer here at all, but there certainly is a level of how good the answer is, and that is what we need to understand and achieve to finalize matters!

Take some time out for this chapter as there are quite a lot of questions we will be going through, and we will look into various possibilities of answers.

The Light Side of the Interview

This might come to you as a surprise, but even the toughest interviews have the tendency to go a little out of the way and bring out a lighter side. Employers and interviewers often prefer adding some random questions into the mix. The answer, regardless of what it may be, will never be right or wrong. If you were to choose 'A' instead of 'B,' it would not matter at all nor would it change the outcome of the circumstances. These are genuinely enjoyable to ask and answer. However, the tone of the answer must be appropriate. You do not wish to answer in a monotonous tone or make things sound gloomy. Show your lighter side and that you, too, are a living person who loves to enjoy other delicacies and luxuries of life apart from working to make a decent living. After all, we earn so that we can spend that money somewhere, right?

Question: "Do you like watching movies on the internet or at a theater?"

Who doesn't like watching movies? I'm quite sure that you too prefer watching movies every now and then. Perhaps one of those big comic-based movies or ones based on true stories. Whichever they may be, let the employer know in a flamboyant way. Step out of the "strictly professional" zone a bit and loosen up. Let your excitement or joy steer your answer to make it sound lively.

Whatever you choose to answer the question above, make it sound like you really mean it. If you are one of those rare groups of people who loathe the idea of watching movies, it is okay to let them know. But you may need to justify your answer almost instantly to make sense. If you say no and follow up with reasons that make little sense, the employers may not be quite happy.

Answer (i): "I love being social and hanging out with my friends. I do love watching movies, not all genres, but I still do tend to enjoy the time and the entertainment value they give. While I do not mind the idea of watching these movies at home, I prefer the big screen. Popcorn, the drink, and good company are just how I like it."

Answer (ii): "I love watching movies all the time. I do not find time to go out much, so I stay at home and watch them on my laptop or television."

Answer (iii): "It's more of a monthly thing for me. I generally do not watch a lot of movies as I am preoccupied with other engagements, but when I do, I prefer to watch them in a theater with my spouse. We always have a good time, especially on the weekends."

Answer (iv): "I am afraid I do not like watching movies at all. I do watch live sports though, and sometimes, the news. I prefer to spend most of my time doing something productive and skillful, like composing music, etc."

Answer (v): "I do not have many friends here in this part of the city. This makes my trip to the theater a little boring. This is why I prefer to watch movies on my laptop. I have all the space I need; I have the food I like, and I have the control to pause, play, rewind, or fast forward whenever I want."

Answer (vi): "I am okay with both, really. To me, the setting does not matter; it is the movie itself that matters. If it is a good movie, I will enjoy it regardless of my location."

All of these answers promote a lively side of you. While there are some answers where things are not as enthusiastic as we would normally see in others, they have provided justifications for their statements. If you take those reasons away, the entire answer becomes quite monotonous and painful to hear.

Do not take the life out of a sentence or an answer by omitting the important bits. Provide clear and complete information. Even when things really do not matter, you are still being judged for the confidence and the way you handle questions or unforeseen circumstances, whether good or bad in nature.

Question: "If you had the option to go back in time, what would you change about your life?"

"I wish I could turn back time and practice a little more to handle such a question more effectively."

Believe it or not, even that would see you go through, although it may not be the kind of answer the interviewer is looking for, so best not to use that.

Be honest with yourself for a moment. Think about all the things that went wrong somewhere in life. We aren't perfect, and we are riddled with errors that continue to haunt us from the past. How dearly would we love to go back in time and correct those errors, right?

For this question, the tone must be moderately excited. Do not overdo it as we are trying to correct something that is wrong in the first place. Here are a few ways you can answer this. Of course, you can modify these answers as you see fit, but the general approach must remain the same.

Answer (i): "The entire prospect of time travel is rather exciting but equally worrisome as well. As long as a few precious people and things remain the same, I would certainly like to go back in time and pay a little more attention to my math classes. It has been my Achilles heel for as long as I can remember. I am not saying that I am horrible with numbers, but I know I could have been quite a lot better."

Answer (ii): "Ah! Time travel. If I had this option with me and I was able to fix something about my life, I would perhaps prevent a few things from happening that harmed me or my loved ones. These could be accidents, mishaps, tragedies, or anything as terrible as you can imagine."

Answer (iii): "Before time traveling, I would memorize some important events in the world of today. I would then go back in time and hopefully invest my money in things like cryptocurrencies, trade markets, and shares that today stand at unimaginable heights. This way, I would be able to reap a hefty profit and lead a life of luxuries and become a prolific investor."

Answer (iv): "I would love to travel back in time and meet my own younger self. I would advise him/her to pay close attention to a few things in life to succeed in the future. I would leave ample notes and clues to suggest that I am not merely a stranger, but an actual version of myself from the future, here to correct all the wrongs I did."

Answer (v): "I would dearly love to travel back in time and ensure I beat myself over being a bully to others. I was a bully for some time before sense hit me and made me realize how wrong I was and how terrible others felt because of me. I would love to correct myself from the early days where it started."

Answer (vi): "I am not too sure if I would like to change anything about my life. I believe life should remain as a big surprise for everyone to deal with head-on. There is no point in living a life if you can go back and change whatever you want whenever you want. Everyone would make mistakes today and then decide to undo them tomorrow."

Every answer from above is correct. All you need is a tone that expresses the emotions, excitement, anguish, and doubts appropriately. That is a sign of a clear communicator, and that is exactly what we are trying to be.

You can come up with your own personalized versions. The answers can be sad or funny, joyous or devastating; it is your call. As long as you do not provide any hints of harming anyone or doing something that is against the law, you are fine. With that said, let's move on to our next question.

Question: "If you wake up tomorrow and you find $10 million to your name, what would you do with that?"

Oh my! $10 million is quite a lot of money. A massive chunk of people would rush to call it a day and settle with early retirement. $10 million would buy you all kinds of luxuries in life, or so it may seem.

If you rush to answer that you would retire, think the answer through. This type of question does test your understanding of life and management skills. Do not take such questions lightly. It is perfectly fine to sound exuberant here if you like, but plan your answer. You may not have the time to focus much on this question if you haven't had any time to prepare for it beforehand.

Tip: *If, for any reason, you haven't prepared your answer beforehand, think of the first few things any human needs. A house, a steady income, and basic facilities. Stick to that and you should be fine!*

Answer (i): "That is quite a lot of money. However, I would not like to spend it senselessly. I would be sensible with that money and try to find ways to double that. First, I would buy a reasonable house. Nothing fancy for now. The rest I would invest in a solid business or buy shares so that I can generate a healthy, steady income. I would continue to work at the same time to meet my expenses on a monthly basis. Once the opportune moment arrives, I would sell my shares and invest in another company. I would continue this cycle to ensure I can double or even triple this figure. That is how I would like my $10 million to be handled."

Answer (ii): "I would be thrilled, to be honest. I would pay off all my debts immediately so that I can begin from scratch. I would use a portion of that money to buy myself a good apartment. I prefer apartments over houses as they are easier to maintain. I would then put the rest of the money, hopefully above half a million dollars, in a savings account to ensure these are generating me some kind of income per month. I am not too confident in investing in shares of businesses as I may not have the right knowledge and experience at this point in time. That would essentially be a risk."

Answer (iii): "If I was to find $10 million in my account for no reason, I would first inquire to find the source to ensure I am not being a victim of fraud here by any chance. If everything seems legitimate, I would then gift my parents half a million dollars, retain half of the remaining amount and donate the rest to some charity. I am sure someone else would need that more than I would. With my share, I would set up a small restaurant or a business that can generate profits for me at the end of each month."

Answer (iv): "To be honest, I have never given that much thought. But, if lady luck was to shine bright and smile on me, I would use some amount to travel the world. I always wanted to do that. This wouldn't be more than 10 percent of the amount. The rest I can keep it in the bank. The reason I would do that is to ensure I do not end up misusing the amount. I would only withdraw it when I have found a potential business venture worth the investment."

Once again, all the answers are perfectly reasonable. Whether you donate the money or keep it to yourself, do not go claiming that you would buy expensive cars, watches, mansions, and real estate as that would essentially cost a little more than the amount you received, and that would be an opening for the interviewer to exploit. You do not wish to be caught in an embarrassing situation where you kick yourself thinking "I should've thought this through."

Question: "What is your greatest fear?"

This is actually quite a common question. Many interviewers have been known to use this question to further examine the kind of candidate they are dealing with. If you are someone who has a phobia of facing a crowded place, you might not be the right fit for a call center or office-based jobs where you are expected to be within a crowded situation every day.

The question isn't necessarily tough, but there are those who tend to make a simple situation more complicated by needlessly talking about difficult situations. Avoid the obvious trap and just stick to basic things. It is absolutely okay to talk about your phobias, such as the phobia of heights, insects, reptiles, and so on. Do not provide a reason for your interviewer to think that you may not be fit for the job, especially if that phobia has quite a lot to do with the job at hand. For someone who cannot speak in public, applying for a trainer's job is beyond possible.

Answer (i): "Well, this might sound funny, but I genuinely find myself uneasy around certain numbers such as the notoriously infamous 666 digits or the number 13. I, for some reason, tend to grow a little insecure when dealing with these numbers. It might be irrational but I am afraid it is there and has been there for quite some time."

Answer (ii): "I am not too sure. There was a time I was afraid of heights. Standing at a high place and staring down would leave me light-headed and dizzy. Recently, I had the chance to skydive, and things have changed completely. Now, I am not sure what scares me. Certainly, there is a fear of failure, but that is common for every human being alive. I guess one day I will find out what scares me now."

Answer (iii): "As it turns out, I do have a phobia or two. I genuinely do not like heights. I am not saying that I feel dizzy all the time. There is a certain level of tolerance that I have been able to maintain. Anything beyond that, and you would find me sweating and feeling funny. The other phobia that I can remember is that of the creepy crawlies. I would leave the room immediately if I saw anything crawling on the floor or on the walls. I cannot stand it, and my instincts take over me."

Answer (iv): "I do hate darkness. I am absolutely terrified of it. Even if I look calm and composed, I know I am screaming at myself to find some source of light to light up the place. To give you an idea of how badly I loathe and fear darkness, I sleep with my lights on. If someone were to turn them off, I would wake up immediately and rush to switch them back on."

Okay! Some rather unusual answers, but then again, the question wasn't usual to begin with. With all said and done, these answers are perfectly justifying the stance of the candidate. It is only human nature to be afraid of something while being perfectly normal with other things being around them. Stay true to your instinct and immediately filter out what seems inappropriate. The rest should flow to you naturally.

Question: "What do you normally do in your spare time?"

This perhaps is the easiest answer of the lot, by a country mile. The reason we claim this to be easy is that it is unique to almost everyone in existence. You might prefer to spend quality time with your friends while the candidate before you prefers to practice playing guitars. The candidate that will come next may be interested in console gaming; the answers will vary from person to person. It is, therefore, quite easy to come up with an answer of your own.

Remember, the interviewer asked you about your *spare time*, and therefore, the answer should not affect your work time at all.

Answer (i): "Well, I am an avid gamer. I find myself quite happy and energetic playing online games. I am rather good at them as I play competitive online games such as COD, Warcraft, and so on. When I have limited spare time, I prefer to sleep it off and rejuvenate myself to ensure I can handle the forthcoming tasks and chores with all my energy and presence of mind. I believe a fresh mind is a key component to ensuring success in whatever you do."

Answer (ii): "I love to work out whenever I have free time. It is a part of my daily schedule to visit the gym and exercise. I am one of those who is quite conscious about their looks and health. While I may not be in the perfect shape yet, I plan on achieving that one day."

Answer (iii): "I am a family guy. I have two kids and a wife, and naturally, my spare time is dedicated to ensuring that we all have a great time. Since the neighborhood we live in is somewhat remote from the city, we often go out on drives and dine out at our favorite restaurants and fast food places. I find it quite a healthy way to connect with my younger ones and spend quality time with my wife and kids at the same time."

Answer (iv): "I rarely get spare time these days. Apart from my main work, I do have other commitments to attend as I am the only one looking after the house. I ensure everything is taken care of, and by the end of the day, the only free time I get is when I am ready to hit the bed after a well-deserved shower."

Questions like these are generally to find out a little more about you as a person, beyond the scope of work. This information may come in handy for the employers at times. For example, knowing that you have kids and are married would suggest that they may need to provide appropriate benefits for family members, where possible. There is no reason to be alarmed and no reason why you should find yourself in a tricky spot. Answer naturally and easily.

The more fluently you answer such questions, the better the impression you leave your interviewer. Regardless of the question, remain easy and maintain an appropriate tone. When needed, use a little hint of exuberance and excitement. Where appropriate, remain formal and concise.

Question: "If you had the chance, what kind of career would you have opted for instead?"

First things first, you must understand that this question does not demand you to name fields related to your current academics and experiences. If you name something that is loosely similar to what you are already doing or applying for, they may consider you a bit of a risk. Ensure that you steer clear of that and choose something completely different, one which would require you to acquire proper degrees, diplomas, or certifications in order to be eligible to pursue. This could be anything you may have ever wanted.

Of course, there is always a possibility that you may be right where you want to be. In that case, you must explain how this field is what you have always dreamed of and are happy to be working for.

Answer (i): "I am quite sure I would not have taken any other career path as I have always dreamed of being a programmer all my life. I am exceptionally good with codes; I am efficient and creative, which serves me with all the advantage I need to make a career out of programming. However, for the sake of discussion, I believe I would have been happy with game development. While it may involve programming, it is a completely separate realm and needs specialized education and experience, one that I do not have nor can acquire without years of study."

Answer (ii): "Tough call, to be honest. I think I would have loved to switch my career and hopefully pursue one in motorsports. I am thrilled by the idea of being in a bucket seat of a car with racing pedigree, a roaring engine, and a track that is laid out for racers to conquer. I am not too sure if that would require proper education, but I am quite certain it requires years of training."

Answer (iii): "My love for games is evident enough. I love to play console games all the time. If I ever had the chance to switch careers, I would opt for game designing. I am creative and love to explore my creativity. I have ideas that I think would pave the way for some massive games, but unfortunately, I do not have the experience nor the knowledge of applying these and converting them into a playable game."

Answer (iv): "I have always fancied the idea of being the face of a news channel. If I had the chance to switch careers, I would have certainly pursued a career as a newscaster. I do love the way they present news and remain calm and composed, even when the worst might have happened. It is also a great way to remain updated with facts and news from around the world. That helps in maintaining a certain charm as the work will never be repetitive, and I would have always dealt with something new and fresh to deliver."

All the answers are designed to ensure they clarify one key element by highlighting the '*if*' factor. This ensures that the interviewer knows you cannot change your career as it would take formal training or education spanning years. This minimizes the chances of you deciding to abandon ship just as something major is about to take place and your services are playing a vital part.

Question: "Where do you see yourself five years from now?"

Well, we are certainly unable to see into the future, and that does dampen things a little for most of us. If you haven't actually planned out what you need to do in life, you might be struck badly by this question. In order to answer this effectively, use the time you have right now and plan out some short-term and long-term goals for your life. Using that information, you should now be in a perfect position to deliver a compelling answer, one that is certain to garner some more points for you.

Your plans do not need to be elaborate; they just need to sound realistic. You cannot go around claiming that you see yourself as a millionaire in five years' time. Sure, there are those who actually were able to do this, but the chances of that happening here are slim. There is no reason why you should stop hoping for the best, but at an interview, hoping for the best is not required. A more realistic approach will garner you the attention you need.

Answer (i): "While it may seem like a lot of time, I am sure five years would just fly past me before I realize it. However, I do have certain plans for myself at a point where I would be leading a good life. I would be able to pay off all my debts; I would hopefully be driving a reasonable car of my own and living in a nice apartment that is close to work. These are some of the goals I wish to achieve, and as long as I continue doing what I am doing right now, I see no reason why I should not be able to convert them into a reality."

Answer (ii): "I have actually given this a fair amount of thought and done all the math, crunched the numbers, and analyzed the situation carefully. Five years from now, I would like to see myself promoted to a good position where I would be earning a lot more compared to today. Sure enough, the position would fetch some perks and benefits as well. I intend to use them to further enhance my living standards for myself and my family."

Answer (iii): "The next five years of my life are a genuine struggle to gain a solid foundation. I hope to see myself as an established professional with reasonable tenure of experience and polished skills. I would certainly like to consider a promotion or two within that period, as it would greatly help me out with my life beyond work."

Answer (iv): "I have my plans to work smartly and prove my worth to my bosses to merit a promotion or two. If achieved, I would ensure I put in all I have to maximize my earnings and minimize my expenditure. By the end of the five-years-long journey, I intend to get married to the love of my life and afford the marriage on my own without bothering any of the parents on either side."

Intriguing, interesting, and thought-provoking. The answers are well thought out and organized. The more you plan, the better you are able to gauge your success. If you have certain plans, you will be able to explain them much more easily. If you haven't already done so, jot down the points and goals, starting now. Once done, start striking off the ones that are far too ambitious, and you should eventually end up with realistic goals. Depending on your potential earnings per month, carry out the calculations, and you should be able to realize which of these are achievable in a certain time.

The exercise is not only important for this interview, but it will also help you out in your own personal life. Think, plan, and execute; that is the order to follow!

If you are intending to gather experience from the company for a few years and then move on to a bigger opportunity that may await you, it is best to keep mum on such points. We do not wish to leave our interviewer or employer with a dilemma on whether to hire us or not based on what you may have just shared.

Question: "Do you prefer being honest and straightforward with your loved ones or would you lie to them to prevent breaking their hearts?"

If you haven't already noticed, this question does have a bit of a trap. The worst thing is that both sides hold equal merits and demerits for you, as a person and as a professional. The question is cleverly asking you to be honest in the first place. Then it asks you, honestly, whether you are the kind of person who would not mind being blunt and straightforward, even if that breaks the heart of a person, or if you would lie, which isn't exactly a great feeling either. It does put you in a bit of a dilemma, doesn't it?

Fortunately, there are ways you can answer such questions without raising any eyebrows. The better news is that these are easier to answer than you might imagine. If you aren't too sure, remain neutral. That is the safest bet to play.

Answer (i): "Well Sir/Madam, that completely depends on who the person is and what exactly is going on for which I am being asked to be honest or lie. If it is something that is genuinely wrong and may end up harming them in any way, I would advise them to refrain from such acts or events. If it is something that isn't as bad, I might even lead with a simple lie, just for the sake of the other person's happiness."

Answer (ii): "If I lie to someone I love, I would not hesitate to lie to anyone else. I genuinely believe it is best to remain honest and straightforward. Sure, the person, on the other hand, may not receive this well at first, but eventually, they will realize it was only for their best. If there are times where you know speaking the truth would cause problems, it is best to try and remain silent on the issue."

Answer (iii): "Speaking as a human being, I would prefer to remain somewhere in the middle. I cannot think of uttering lies nor can I think of harming anyone's ego or happiness. I would take a silent route out of the situation. As a professional, I would ensure I remain true to my obligations and duties toward the organization itself. If needed, I would not hesitate to lie for them, just to save the face value of the organization."

Answer (iv): "It depends on what the situation is. If it is a personal matter between me and my loved ones, I would not hesitate in telling them things as they are, even if it ruins the mood. Being a professional, I do believe it is best to be as honest as possible. This eases the communication between all employees and promotes transparency and trust. If I was to lie to anyone within the company or for the company, it would damage the trust and eventually harm me and the firm itself."

It doesn't matter how you handle it, but it is certainly recommended to ensure you distinguish your personal life from your work life within the answer. Let the interviewer know you are there for them and are willing to remain quiet where possible.

Also, ensure that you draw a line in the sand as we saw in the fourth answer. This lets the employer know that you are a man of your word and that you value integrity for yourself and for the company. Strike a balance and lead with that!

Question: "Do you prefer to work on a team or lead the team instead?"

We begin with a tip for you right away. Always handle such questions with care. If you are wondering why, then switch places and think as an interviewer would think. Analyze the question now and you will immediately see why this question needs special care.

If you are applying for a job that normally revolves around teamwork, it is obviously a plus point that you prefer working as a member of the team, but staying limited to that would bar you from leadership roles. These are the roles performed by an individual who is leading the charge. If you stick to the latter alone, you might not be a good fit at all. So how do you handle such a question? Fear not as we shall look into various answers for this as well.

Answer (i): "I have been a team player throughout my professional life. I have worked on various teams and have learned how to fully operate matters. It is through this experience that I was able to gain valuable lessons and learned how to lead teams as well. In an ideal situation, a good team would have a good team leader and vice versa. But that is rarely the case. I have learned that in order to be an effective leader, you first need to work as a member of the team to fully understand matters and then lead the team once you have mastered the art."

Answer (ii): "That would be easy. I generally prefer working as a one-man show. In all fairness though, this is only made possible if the team that works under me is performing its duties well. Through the leadership qualities and skills that I have come to inherit from my experience as a team member, I know how things work on the basic level and can guide the team to ensure an error-free working environment. I can ensure that each member of the team learns how to take responsibility and tries to give their maximum by appreciating them and praising them every now and then."

Answer (iii): "While I would love to be in a position where I can lead as a one-man show, I believe it requires experience, training, and knowledge before I can earn that position. That is only possible through teamwork. Being a member of the team, I would ensure that I work hard and understand all the nitty gritties of the job before taking a leap forward."

These answers are more than justifiable and just about right in terms of length. If you needlessly stretch the answer, you might find yourself interrupted by the interviewer's next question.

Speak briefly but with intent and purpose. Know what you need to convey and do so effectively.

Question: "How do you handle pressure and stress?"

When you are in a working environment, there are all kinds of pressure and stress that will mount on you. While most of the time it may be negligible, there will be times where it will all feel far too much for you to handle. In such cases, quite a lot of employees end up having a nervous breakdown, fits of rage, and might even become an immediate threat to others nearby.

The internet is brimming with videos and articles where people have lost their tempers and cool, and they have gone on to damage the equipment and cause chaos and panic within the workplace. Needless to say, their fate is quite obvious. With the increasing number of such reports pouring in from all directions, employers and interviewers are taking precautions to ensure they only hire people who can hold their composed nature and remain calm when the going gets really tough.

You might be the calmest guy on the block, but when faced with such a question, you may feel lost for words. The best strategy? Well, you have already picked up this book, haven't you? That's half your work done already as we shall look into the answers and see how we can tackle these questions. The other half is completely dependent on how you manage to answer the question when the actual time arrives.

Answer (i): "I have been known as one of the calmest guys on the team wherever I have worked so far. I take pride in the fact that I normally don't feel pressured or stressed because of my work. Part of it is because I always arrive at work knowing that I am to expect the worst pressure and stress today. This helps me in creating the room I need mentally to keep my calm and composed nature at the ready. The other part is how I manage my work during work hours. I never let things go past deadlines, and I always ensure I deliver on time. This helps me maintain my calm and composed nature and stay away from succumbing to pressure."

Answer (ii): "I do understand that work can, at times, be very demanding. I do have a family, and it is said that family people are easier prey for pressure and stress. This is why I keep with me one of those small pressure-relieving toys to ensure I never go past my threshold and take the stress out easily."

Answer (iii): "Pressure and stress are natural. If I worry too much about these elements, sure enough, I will fail. This is why I never focus on things that may cause pressure and make me do work that is substandard in nature. I am not easily distracted by pressure or stress, so I wouldn't worry too much about that at all."

All of these answers are fine, even the second one. There are people who genuinely suffer from ailments that may cause them to have fluctuating blood pressure levels. If needed, you can carry those soft and squishy cubes or spheres and use them whenever you feel the pressure mounting up. One other way of handling pressure is to speak with colleagues. You can mention that too as an answer if needed.

Do not let your employers feel that you would succumb to the pressure. Let them know that you have what it takes to handle the kind of pressure they may have at the workplace by carrying out your duties on time. If everything is sorted within the timeframe, there is no reason to be worried or feel pressured, right?

Question: "What makes you feel uncomfortable?"

This question is perilously close to the one we viewed earlier. Can you guess which question that was? It was the one where we discussed our fears and phobias. This question is something a little less scary.

Anything—a person or situation—that makes you feel a little uneasy or uncomfortable would fall here. This does not include anything you may fear. You might be terrified of heights, but you are uneasy on the ground in the middle of a large crowd. While you won't fall unconscious or find it hard to breathe, you just find it annoying to be in the middle of such a crowd where everyone is on the phone, talking, laughing, screaming, and bumping into each other. These are the kind of things you are expected to answer.

Once again, do take care in answering this question as some of it might be related to the work itself. With that in mind, let us look at some possible versions. Modify them where you wish and come up with your version of the answer to further help you practice these.

Answer (i): "I will not deny the fact that I get somewhat uncomfortable when I am facing strangers individually. I am perfectly fine in a crowded situation, but when alone with a stranger for any given reason, I feel uncomfortable as starting a conversation is somewhat tough. Although I have worked on my social skills, it is still something that leaves me in a little uncomfortable."

Answer (ii): "I am a natural talker. I love socializing, but there are things that continue to haunt me for some reason. One of them is the prospect of saying 'no' to someone. I am not comfortable with the idea of saying no to people when I know I can actually help them out. This is both good and at times bad on my part. I am working on learning how to easily say no, and things have started to improve now."

Answer (iii): "I do not find myself comfortable around people who are drinking as I genuinely hate drinking habits. I do not drink nor do I encourage others to do so. Unfortunately, there are quite a lot of friends that I know who continue to drink, and at times, I am around when they do. As uncomfortable as I may get, I have learned to accept things the way they are."

You can come up with as many versions of answers as you like. Ideally, begin with at least three versions, if not more, and practice. Remember to use the tone to emphasize words and aspects of your answer. Provide the interviewer with a feeling that you are genuinely disturbed or feel uneasy about things that tend to annoy or bother you. If you are able to do that, even the dullest answer will sound quite a lot better than you might imagine. If you don't believe that, record your version of the answer twice. The first time, use a monotonous tone, and in the second go, use an appropriate tone. Review the audio and hear the difference.

All of these questions require you to practice a few key components:

- Tone
- Fluency
- Confidence
- Content
- Clarity
- Pace

Get any of these wrong and your answer will immediately lose its charm. Do your best to answer these as they come. Use the time that you have productively and come up with various versions if you need to. These will help you in the future as well, in case you decide to switch workplaces or be interviewed for a possible promotion.

To Sum Up the Chapter

We went through quite a lot of answers in this chapter. We primarily focused on questions that are sometimes uncommon or not expected. These questions are genuine and do have a tendency of showing up just when you thought you had everything covered.

Designed to test your quick responses, logical reasoning, and behavior when faced with such questions, these are used by interviewers around the world to further confirm the candidate's nature and understand the potential employee better. This helps them in making the all-important decision of extending an invitation to work or rejecting the profile altogether.

How you answer these questions will always be up to you. The book provides you with a general overview of how these questions are handled. It is your own responsibility to ensure you practice these answers as much as possible to make them sound more natural and realistic. Ensure that you keep your answers brief and sweet. Do not add information that may be deemed unnecessary or vague in nature.

Use your confidence through positive body language and through your words. Be careful and mindful of what you say as interviewers and potential employers are ready to focus on things that may raise their eyebrows in interest or confusion. Do not overshoot things nor complicate easy questions with answers that never seem to end. Know when to begin and where to stop; the rest should be a walk in the park for you.

Now we have covered all the bases and regions that needed covering, but what about certain questions that sound slightly offensive, too personal, or discriminatory? How would you handle those? Should you answer them at all? Our next chapter will provide you with detailed insight into how you can handle these tricky situations and what you need to do in order to avoid a rather awkward situation.

Chapter 8: The Illegal Questions!

You read that right! As unfortunate as this may sound, there are employers who tend to ask questions that are not only unethical and personal in nature, they are declared illegal across many countries, if not all across the world.

Employers have been reported by masses for asking questions that have nothing to do with the job. While most of the people will sit in awkward silence or just deliver an answer, there are specific things you must be aware of and should know at all times.

Employers, big or small, must obey the law and adhere to the general rules set out by the firm and the law in place for employees within the specific state or country. What kind of questions might these be? Let us find out in detail. We will not be diving deep into explaining what the question is. We are instead more interested in understanding our rights and using them in an answer appropriately.

This Is Not Relevant

Indeed! If an employer or interviewer asks you questions that are far too personal in nature, you have the right to say no and move on with the rest of the interview. Interviewers are human beings as well. That means there is always room for error on their part. If a question is posed to you and has words or a meaning that may seem inappropriate, you can use the classic way to dodge the bullet while maintaining composure and character. How? Here's an example!

Question: "Are you interested in working with men?"

Sure enough, the question seems to be raising eyebrows. Perhaps, the interviewer was unable to find the right way to put the question.

Answer: "Sorry, but if you are trying to ask whether I can work alongside men, I am absolutely capable of doing so. I do not mind who I work with as a professional."

Not only will you dodge the bullet, but you might also be able to create a good impression here as well. You did not react oddly, and you still answered the question. Most likely, the interviewer will apologize for misstating the question and the awkwardness will end right there and then.

This example is perfectly understandable. We all make mistakes, and it can happen to the best of us at the worst of times. Be sure to give the benefit of the doubt to everyone, even your potential employer.

Now, we shall move on to a few questions that are both awkward and offensive in nature. These are deliberately put forth either out of ignorance or hatred. Handling such questions will not be easy and will require you to have all the confidence and determination to hold your ground and remind them of the right cause, without being threatening, abusive, or harsh in voice and tone.

Question: "Were your parents born within the States?"

Even if you aren't in the United States of America—say the interview is being conducted in London, England—no employer has the right to pose this question to you. This information will serve them with no purpose nor reflect the nature of the work you are capable of doing. If you encounter this question or any such question of the same meaning, here's how to answer it.

Answer: "My apologies, sir/madam, but neither this question nor its answer has anything to do with my skills and ability to perform my duties. I would appreciate it if you could ask me questions related to the opportunity at hand."

As mentioned earlier, it is perfectly okay to take a stand for your rights. You have neither used a threatening tone nor replied harshly. You just evaded a chaotic situation and alerted the employer/interviewer that they may have stepped over the line here.

This is something not many people understand. There are certain rules and regulations laid out by the government that all employers and employees must follow. Unless the job requires research and data collection, you are not bound by any law to answer this question. This may lead to discrimination and other ill factors such as that.

Your best practice would be to refer to rules and regulations that are normally available on various platforms in order to fully understand the limitations set by the law.

Question: "Is English your native language?"

This question may be asked to you if you are someone who has an accent that is different or may have roots from other countries. We live in a world where every country has people living in it who may or may not have been born and raised there. Asking them whether English is their first language or not is yet another way to discriminate against them.

Unless the job specifically requires people who speak English as their native language, like in the case of call center jobs, no employer or interviewer has the right to ask you this question nor are you bound by any law to answer this question. Once again, we need to use professionalism and some words to evade the seemingly awkward and provocative situation.

Answer: "I do apologize if I sound different, but I can assure you this has nothing to do with my skills or my performance on the job."

English is a language that has hundreds of accents. People from all over the world speak it in various accents, and believe it or not, the ones who have learned English as a second language have greater chances of writing and speaking more accurately than you might imagine. Judging them on accent alone is nothing short of discrimination then. Everyone should be respected, regardless of their ethnic background, and only their merit should be judged instead of their religion or political beliefs, accents or skin tone.

If you give in to the question, you are effectively allowing the interviewer to exploit the leniency further, and you might soon be facing questions that are far too offensive for you to handle. It is best to draw the line in the sand early on and avoid confrontation at all costs.

Question: "What religion do you follow?"

Once again, religion has nothing to do with how you operate, work, and interact with others. Unless you are applying at a church, a mosque, or a temple, religion should have no connection or relation to the job in question.

It is observed that a number of employers and interviewers tend to breach this general code of conduct that is in place for them set either by the organization itself or the law. Since most of the candidates who are applying are already under pressure, they tend to carry on answering these questions.

If you are comfortable in answering this question, do so. If you feel the slightest hint of doubt, you have every right to excuse yourself from answering this question by using the same kind of reply as we saw earlier.

Answer: "My apologies, but I do not see the correlation between the two. My religion or religious belief should have no effect on how I carry out my duties."

Remain calm and composed. Do not give in to the temptation to raise your tone of voice or show your authority. This would only invite trouble as there is every likelihood that your voice is being recorded. This can then be used against you in a court of law as a threatening tone. Even in such tough circumstances, you will need to remain calm. If you cannot withstand such questions, you can always end the interview and walk away. If so, use this as your closing answer.

Answer: "I sincerely apologize, but I fail to see how I can possibly work positively in an organization that is judging people based on their religious beliefs and ethnic backgrounds. It was lovely meeting you, and I wish you the best of luck."

You are the guardian of your own self-esteem. There are hundreds of other opportunities out there; leaving this one should not bring you down. Stand up for your rights should you be subjected to such questions.

Question: "Do you normally go out with people from work?"

This might come to you as a surprise, but this question is actually more common than you might expect. The chances of you facing this question are rare at best, and it is generally the female candidates who are subjected to questions such as this.

This is an indication that you are perhaps in an organization that does not necessarily pay close attention to the employees and might have people who have a history of harassing others. Should you remain silent on this matter, you might be walking into a potential risk. The moment you face this question, respond appropriately, using the same professional tone as we have practiced thus far and remind them of the limits.

There are certain rules and regulations in place, as per the law, that protect every citizen and employee from such cases. After you have dealt with the interviewer, approach the higher authority or contact the local police or a lawyer to discuss the matter further.

While this can be done after you are done with the interview, what you need to do during the interview is respond somewhat like this:

Answer: "I do find that question both disturbing and uncourteous in nature. This neither reflects my professional capabilities nor my competitiveness. I would appreciate it if you can avoid such questions moving forward as I am not at all comfortable nor liable to answer that."

Strict, to the point, and concise. It is more than enough for you to do. This should serve any sane employer and interviewer with a warning that you are offended and that they have clearly stepped over the line of professionalism and ethics.

Remaining calm is advisable; remaining quiet is not. Ensure that you provide the authorities with the information and let them know how such questions can affect the females within society. While you may have gone to seek a job opportunity, and most likely ended up losing it, it is for the best. Your integrity and professionalism come first.

You may wish to seek opportunities within another firm that respects your privacy and your beliefs. There is no point in pursuing a job opportunity within an organization that clearly has no regard for the safety or welfare of the potential employees or the law itself.

Question: "How old are you?"

Did you know that no employer has any right to ask you for your age? Unless you are someone who looks far too young, and they clarify that they need some proof of age, they are neither allowed nor encouraged by any law to ask you for your age.

The only reason the employer may ask you for your age is to check whether you are above the legal minimum age to apply for the said job or under the maximum cut-off age set by the organization. Apart from these, there is no reason why your interviewer/employer should inquire about this aspect.

Needless to say, as usual, you will use a friendly tone and let your employer know how age does not affect the way you operate. Try and see if you can come up with your own version of the answer, without breaching the boundaries of ethics and losing your temper. To give you an example, here is one way to answer such a question:

Answer: "My age does not reflect nor alter my ability to perform my duties. The nature of the job requires me to be on merit, and I can assure you, my age has nothing to do with it, nor does it give you an insight into my experience and knowledge."

While it is generally observed that people happily end up answering this question, it is also observed that those who do have no idea that such questions are simply not allowed by the law. If you have also just learned about this today, ensure that you do thorough research for every job opportunity moving forward.

Concluding the Chapter

Interviews are seen as a highly formal event that we go through before acquiring the job we wish to get. These are seen as moments where we sell our skills and expertise to the highest bidder. But just because we are 'selling' our professionalism does not mean we have no rights, and it should not be mistaken as our weakness for others to exploit.

Whether you are applying at big companies or the polar opposite of those, you are protected by quite a number of laws that are constantly in place for every employer, interviewer, and organization to follow. No one is above the law and hence, you have every right to answer some questions perfectly well while avoiding the ones that are derogatory, discriminatory, or downright offensive in nature. Do not give in to the temptation of answering these in a confrontational manner. If you lose your cool, you not only lose your potential job application, but you also lose your legal ground as the interviewer can press charges against you as well.

There are quite a few more questions that you can find on the internet. Ensure that you give them a look and prepare your answers accordingly to what we have learned and seen here. It is always better to be ready and knowledgeable than to try to answer things that should not have been asked in the first place.

The law guards your right as an employee/candidate, and therefore, the institutions should ensure strict adherence to the law. While most of the organizations continue to do so, there are a few that tend to overlook such matters. It is, therefore, our duty to remind them of their legal duties and not react or erupt while we do that.

With that said, we have completed everything there is to learn about how to come up with brilliant answers that are imaginative, creative, and purpose-driven. Use your knowledge and answers wisely by choosing the right words. While this chapter gave you insight into the legal grounds, the remainder of the book has hopefully provided you with sufficient knowledge to digest.

Draw your inspirations accordingly, and lead the charge by example. Clench your victory as it awaits you. All that stands between you and a perfect job is a set of right answers. Now you have the tools and guidance as well!

Conclusion

This has been one entertaining, informative, and productive journey. From being an exciting prospect to a fully taught and ready candidate, we have gone through the highs and lows of the matter that is involved in interviews.

"Interview Answers" has hopefully served the purpose that it sought to in the first place. The pure intention was to provide every candidate with a perfect guide to understand how the much-dreaded and feared interview is handled. Not only did we briefly touch upon matters that are explained in detail within the other books, but we dove down into the never-ending depths of the answers themselves.

We discovered how various answers leave various impressions on the employer. We saw how using the wrong words and tone can devastate an otherwise perfect effort. Throughout the book, we assumed that the candidate has all the basic requirements fulfilled. These mostly include the educational requirements and understanding of the skills involved in order to be shortlisted. The rest comprised of answers that help you achieve the job you so dearly seek out.

Answering questions is one thing, but answering them in an interview is a completely different game altogether. Since we already feel the pressure and stress that the interview generally brings, we may end up faltering and losing our perfect opportunity. This book ensures that the candidates have all the help they need to understand the smaller details and work their way up accordingly to be able to answer these questions impressively.

Interviews are all about testing the mettle of the candidate in question. The interviewers demand you answer the questions that are expected, and sometimes, they may throw questions that are least expected. In either case, remain calm and composed and focus on the question asked before providing the answer.

It is imperative that you use the time you have before the interview to carry out all the tasks before considering yourself ready for the interview. While you may have the documents in order and the pictures that may be needed, the biggest hurdle, and the one that is overlooked by almost every other person, is the practice.

The more you practice speaking and applying the knowledge you have gained within this book, the easier it will be for you to answer these questions when the actual interview arrives. Do not let fear control you nor should you allow the intimidation to build up. Remain focused and confident and answer your questions accordingly.

Throughout the book, we mentioned that confidence is the key element for a largely successful interview. Only through finding confidence will you muster up a perfect answer and deliver. The content and the tone are secondary, but important nonetheless.

Choose your answers carefully and provide concise information that is true to the best of your knowledge and avoid making comments or speaking about matters that may leave a negative impression.

Know the limits of the law that each employer and interviewer must observe. Should any of them breach this fine line, you can use a professional and friendly tone to remind them that they have stepped over the line without actually using these words. We have seen in detail how we can answer these questions accordingly. All it takes is practice and a bit of confidence to stand true to yourself and your course.

If in the future, you need to revisit the book, be sure to keep a pen and paper ready and take notes down where possible. These will greatly help you throughout your life as interviews are not just a one-time thing. These do have the tendency of coming back and finding you sitting within the chair of a candidate and having someone else interview you yet again.

Be confident, be positive. Use a tone that is natural. Sound happy where needed and sound concerned when possible. Do not be intimidated by any of these questions. Answer at your will and answer well.

Nothing in life is impossible; all it takes is a soul that is willing to achieve what many have failed to.

Let this be a journey for you to explore and remember. The knowledge that you have acquired here will last you a lifetime. You can use these answers in almost every part of your life, regardless of the field of work you may be involved in. Use the knowledge wisely, use your words carefully, and practice as much as you can.

There is no such thing as the 'last' interview. You never know when you might need to undergo another interview one more time. Keep your confidence up, pay close attention to what the interviewer asks, and provide answers that are spot on and relevant. Overstretching answers will serve you with nothing. All you might be able to garner is a yawn from the interviewer or an interruption to suggest he/she is clearly not interested in you.

Avoid exposing your weaknesses by identifying them and taking corrective action today. Age-old habits may take some time to change, but at least you can easily state that you have already started working to make things better.

Never shy away from boasting about your key strengths, and highlight them whenever possible. Provide relevant examples if you can to further support your claim and ensure that your employer understands you know what you are talking about.

Finally, if you found this book useful in any way, a review on Amazon is always appreciated!

Made in the USA
Middletown, DE
17 May 2020